FROM HERE TO THERE

Africa Migration Report Poetry Anthology Series

From Here to There

101 Poems on African and African Diasporic Migration

Edited by Nandi Jola and Omobola Osamor

Civic ♥ Leicester

First published in Great Britain in 2025 by
CivicLeicester
y. https://www.youtube.com/user/CivicLeicester
f. https://www.facebook.com/CivicLeicester
CivicLeicester@gmail.com

ISBN-978-1-0682210-3-3

Dedicated to all who are looking for home.

CONTENTS

Introduction   xi

The Beautiful Journey Oluwaseyi Adebola   1

jewels lost at sea Abiola Agbaje   2

Ncuti Looks Back Jim Aitken   3

Port Harcourt Rina Malagayo Alluri   4

Blessing Rina Malagayo Alluri   5

A Nameless Corpse Eavesdropping Driss Amjich   6

Bloom Driss Amjich   7

A Distant World Gordon Anjili   8

Emigrants Gordon Anjili   9

A Migrant Yemi Atanda   10

Journeys Beyond Borders Amisah Bakuri   11

Nighttime Antje Bothin   13

what is africa Yasmin S Brown   14

Strategic Unification Yasmin S Brown   16

African Origins M. Chambers   17

African Exile M. Chambers   19

No Buts... (Universal Declaration of Human Rights?)   20
Barrington Gordon

A Dreadful Day Zainab M. Hassan   22

Breath of Identity Zainab M. Hassan   24

Back To Where You Came From Zita Holbourne   26

Reaped Dreams Ugwuja Emmanuel Ifeanyichukwu   27

Covered by Prayer Zan V. Johns   28

Nostalgia Nandi Jola   29

Black Women Nandi Jola   30

Victim of Tribalism Samuel Julius Habakkuk Kargbo   31

Ramshackle Boats Samuel Julius Habakkuk Kargbo   33

you're always going Anton Krueger   35

from here to there Thulani Mahlangu   36

Where I Am From Thulani Mahlangu   37

Más que la luna al sol Esther Mamadou   39

Grace on the move Monica Manolachi   40

Delivery Service Monica Manolachi   41

To Lina Leonora Masini   42

Only Berberè? Leonora Masini   44

Preparations for the Voyage to Lampedusa   46
                                    Octavia McBride-Ahebee
1822/2014 Octavia McBride-Ahebee   47

The Isthmus That Splits Us Karuna Mistry   48

Perspectives (Home from Home) Karuna Mistry   49

Country Marks Jenny Mitchell   50

Looking at the Benin Bronzes Jenny Mitchell   51

I Am Somali Nasra Dahir Mohamed   52

Why We Left Nasra Dahir Mohamed   54

The B(lack)ody As a Map to Self Mariam Mohammed   55

From where do I come? Mariam Mohammed   56

Echoes of A Migrant's Ritual Fauziyatu 'Fauzi' Moro   57

Africa's Children Remind Mugwambani   58

Footsteps of Our Ancestors Remind Mugwambani   60

st georges walks into a pub Ambrose Musiyiwa   61

There Will Always Be One More Thing Ambrose Musiyiwa   62

Old/Lonely/Homeless Francis Muzofa   72

Serengeti Gazelles Francis Muzofa   73

Complicity J.O. Neill   75

From God to Dust Jana van Niekerk   76

A Journey Full Circle Dike Nwosu   80

not quite knowing our station Dike Nwosu   83

Lamentations Takunda G Nyika   85

Haunted Takunda G Nyika   87

Don't Surprise Me Europe   Joseph C Ogbonna   88

Japa Quagmire   Joseph C Ogbonna   89

They Were Once Demigods   Tanure Ojaide   90

Remembering Edinburgh, 1979   Tanure Ojaide   91

Remembering   Dike Okoro   92

Another Man's Land   Victor Ola-Matthew   94

King Samba of Wazombia   Omotayo Olaoye   97

Strange Noises from the Embassy   Omotayo Olaoye   98

Dear Mother   Frank Olunga   99

Inside a Euro-Tunnel   Alexander Opicho   101

Tomorrow on today's plate   Omobola Osamor   102

You Threw Yourself Away   Omobola Osamor   103

A Refugee's Prayer   Omobola Osamor   104

First Time   Annette Pateman   105

The Search   Elly Ray   106

Homeland Strays   Elly Ray   107

Sibboleth   Eric Rugara   108

Refugee Woman   Mudadi Saidi   109

Blood and Sugar of Home   Deborah Saki   111

A New City   Deborah Saki   113

Long Live Livelihood   Partha Sarkar   115

Innocents Are Either Dead or Escapists   Partha Sarkar   116

A Promise of Hope   James Sentiba   117

Swamp Song   James Sentiba   118

as long as   Ndaba Sibanda   119

s(t)(c)reams of splendor   Ndaba Sibanda   121

Kunta Kinte   Palmwine Sounds   122

The Green, Red, Black and Gold   Palmwine Sounds   123

immigrant generation   Cindy Steward   124

it matters   Cindy Steward   126

Intergenerational Trauma   SuAndi   127

Rights Abridged   Sheila Thadani   130

Slaughter of An African King Sheila Thadani   132

Until Again Goma is Free! Patrick Kapuya Tshiuma   134

The Long Way Home Patrick Kapuya Tshiuma   136

Zulu Girl In Rotterdam Philisiwe Twijnstra   138

The Prisoner Ijeoma Victory Ejme   140

So Much For So Little Ijeoma Victory Ejme   141

If only... Faresi Yasini   142

African Woman Dreams of Freedom Faresi Yasini   143

Mimi Fly's Rich Gorrety Yogo   144

You Need To Let It Go! Furaha Youngblood   145

Adrift Furaha Youngblood   147

Who Will Dare to Think Outside the Box? Kathy Zwick   149

Contributors   151

Acknowledgements   161

About the Africa Migration Report Poetry Anthology Series   164

INTRODUCTION

Sawubona!

A Zulu word that literally translates to 'I/we see you', and which is used as a greeting, a hello.

In this anthology, this very simple word opens our eyes so we see each other as brothers and sisters with no borders, on shared journeys, intertwined in dualities of shared love, hope and despair, joy and grief, hardship and relief, on a shared quest for life, for a place to call home, and for a liveable future.

Look at Ncuti.

Embody his spirit.

And as you read each poem, echoing the rhythm and, at times, the rhymes of dispossession and displacement, keep walking with him.

Home transcends brick and mortar.

Home encompasses the familiarity of those who get us, the cushions we rest on.

Familiarity, blessed familiarity.

But what happens when home is torn apart by war and conflict? When home is no longer safe? When you are forced to flee in search of safety or for a place where you can be yourself in all your glory or a place where you can simply be you?

What happens when poverty or discrimination denies you the ability to thrive? When survival, your survival, and the survival of those around you is not guaranteed?

We are poets of a generation that will not remain silent.

We cut across borders, fences, checkpoints, immigration control. We swam the Atlantic. Our brothers and sisters drown. We survive to tell them we see their eyes look at us as we cross over. In Lampedusa. In the English Channel. In the human zoos in France. In slave markets in Libya. In the Darién Gap. At the US/Mexico border. In the desert. In Algeria. In Egypt, Morocco, Tunisia …

Homeland strays. The isthmus that split us is very thin. An illusion. A mere ghost of empire. It is the beast we each confront in our writing, re-writing, telling and re-telling of the cosmos, folklores, lives and tales of the living, of our ancestors and soon-to-be ancestors. An archive that refuses our people's mis-education and destruction. Poetry is as ancient as our chromosomes. Each of us.

Sawubona!

Nandi Jola and Omobola Osamor,
Belfast, Northern Ireland, and Chicago, USA,
November 2025

Oluwaseyi Adebola
The Beautiful Journey

A time not too far away,
is where I want to be.
It is as beautiful as it is obscure
yet my soul longs for it
like an eagle longs for the sky.
Though I stand in pseudo-paradise,
I clear my mind of lazy haze
lest complacency become my lot
and I dwell in this place forever.
I pick myself up resolutely
from my bed of beauty
and trudge relentlessly
towards an even more beautiful place,
a land that is pretty and fair
where ravens of fortune shall bear me up
and springs of peace soothe my soul.
Someday,
when I get there,
I'll rest awhile
before picking my mind up
once again
to begin a journey
towards a land that's even prettier
and clearer
and not too far away,

Abiola Agbaje
jewels lost at sea

sea of migration
migration scare because we ran from starvation
starvation that killed mama's first son
mama's first son, who was supposed to take us out of poverty
poverty that slid down generations
generations of enslaved and dispossessed landowners
landowners who are now beggars on their own land
land once rich with milk and honey
honey so rich it glittered like gold and expensive jewels
jewels now being lost at sea
sea of migration with siren songs of hope
hope that one day we will reach the promised land
promised land of colonizers who enslaved our ancestors
ancestors condemned, in their graves, to watch us
watch us voluntarily walk into shackles
shackles held by people who do not see us as human

Jim Aitken
Ncuti Looks Back

Of course, some people ask me
about being born in Rwanda
and about the Hutus and the Tutsis
once they know I came from there.

I tell them little, for I was little
at the time, a toddler of a few years.
We fled the genocide and came to Scotland,
first to Edinburgh and then over to Fife.

We fled genocide and found racism.
My mother told me, "Get on with it."
And I did. And they grew to love me
just as I always knew they would.

At the Royal Conservatoire in Glasgow
studying there, I soon discovered that
the Hutus and Tutsis met their match
with fans of Rangers and fans of Celtic.
I graduated in acting and headed to Dundee,
to the Dundee Rep Theatre.
Three strangers attacked me once
and broke my jaw. Yes, I got on with it
and got a titanium jaw instead.

I don't want to boast, but I have performed
at the Globe, starred in Sex Education and Barbie
and have just become the fourteenth Doctor Who,
the fourth Scottish Doctor to date. And later

This year, I will perform at the National Theatre
as Algernon Moncrieff in Oscar Wilde's great play.
Not at all bad for a lad from Nyarugenge, Kigali,
and they are all so proud of me back home there.

Yes, I am an African migration success story
and a success story for Scotland as well
and all I want, all I have ever wanted, is to be
happy inside, inside my beautiful black skin.

3

Rina M. Alluri
Port Harcourt

a street without a destination
small cluster of bungalows
huddled together
full of promise

keeping each other warm
rice fields far away, cassava close by
houses once filled with highlife
left abandoned

Biafra War air raids
forcing rivers of the
Niger Delta to meet
post-colonial fears

buses crammed
not knowing where to go
people traded people for prosperity
Port Harcourt exodus

abundance a curse
earth holding the oil
machines could not keep up
skin soaked with soot

they would later return to homes
that were no longer theirs
freshly painted with
the red blood of war

Rina M. Alluri
Blessing

leaving home every morning at dawn
passing traffic at Oyo Road junction
greeting vendors balancing bread baskets on their heads
as the stench of gasoline stains the Ibadan air

clutching thin white napkins,
she stands in a hot kitchen
frying plantains, cautious of spitting oil,
her wrapper prints camouflage the grease

serving children in air-conditioned living rooms,
she had rocked them to sleep
when they were babies,
she loved them like her own

Driss Amjich
A Nameless Corpse Eavesdropping

Hey,
you

you illegal beings,
you have no place in this station.

Curs,
commence the liberation mission

round them all up
stuff them into covert buses
dump them far from the cities of light
to the south
to the eastern borders
far from the lands of blondes and redheads.

Oh, esteemed liberation leader,
what shall we do with this decomposing corpse?

Tell the press we sent it to the morgue,
then toss it in the trash
where it rightfully belongs
with all those who occupy public property
or resist the privatization of our pristine oasis waters.

Let it be known:
No mercy for those who obstruct Capital
or oppose the influx of foreign investments
or the siphoning of external loans.
Even the northern farmers,
those who disperse the bounties
hidden from the populace;
even the southern neighbours,
those who raised customs fees.

If it were up to me,
the liberation commander,
I'd throw them all into landfills
with the rotting remains of the nameless black corpse.

Driss Amjich
Bloom

The same day all plans crumbled.
The same day I crumbled.

A kiss to the eyes,
An image of no sleep,
Atop a scene,
Before a dark screen.

Sitting on a brown plastic stool.

Anxious,
About an influence and a bloom.

Gordon Anjili
A Distant World

A distant world I know too well
From lofty mountain to the dell,
Replete with priceless, precious gems,
Imbued with legendary names,
Cooled by the soothing mountain air,
And heated by the desert flare.

I cannot tell what ails this world:
So rich, yet suppliant; proud yet gnarled!

Dear countrymen beg in the streets,
Others drudge in survival feats.
On public media, godlings spew
Messages that paint a rosy hue:
Each day is better than the last;
Despite sabotage, growth is fast!

Gordon Anjili
Emigrants

In winter, swallows fly to warmer climes.
In summer, some return, and others stay.
They cannot leave the warm and tempting clime
And thrills of a canty refulgent day.

The robin never flees the milder clime
But is well-schooled in coping with the cold.
To him, all seasons are sweet and the same.
Nothing exists that one has not been told.

Like robins, we stayed. Like swallows, they left.
And some returned to their old summer nests.
We fete and applaud them as patriots true,
And scoff at those who remain foreign guests.

Yemi Atanda
A Migrant

Roving on time's wheel,
Whence I come, thence I go;
On this that had been trodden,
A familiar road, yet forgotten,
Or the one that's in pursuance of life,
Of wild-goose chase in the wind,
Like a droplet of water in a river
Flowing in the direction of no recourse,
As the electrons in meandering collision,
In the ambiguity of atoms, serenaded in twists;
For claiming the right in a blight,
And still seeking for a space to be
Its lord, while slipping on gliding grip
Of emptiness in the air!

Amisah Bakuri
Journeys Beyond Borders

Under the skies,
Migrants from Africa, our stories.
Mothers and fathers' dream.
Siblings await, making schemes.

The past, a journey of trials and tears,
Shackled by history's weighty fears.
Hope, hope ignites in resilient hearts,
Navigating uncharted paths.

Encountering faces and challenges unknown,
In lands afar, sometimes prejudice is sown.
Our presence sparks questions, sparks a dance,
A fragile trance.

From our shores to distant lands,
Seeking refuge with trembling hands.
A welcome or a shun,
Boundaries drawn.

Various stakeholders call,
Yet, actions are small.
Voices raised.
Yet, progress delayed.

Debates arise.
Migrants' fates hang in the skies.
Nations grapple with policies fraught,
Balancing compassion with walls of thought.

African Diasporic communities unite.
Demanding justice, demanding rights.
Yet challenges loom, obstacles vast.
A huge contrast.

The past, a burden. The present, a storm.
Resilience, a glimmer, a form.
Promises untold.
Stories unfold.
In unity, in strength, rising above,

Embracing the journey, embracing love.
In destiny's weave,
Courage. Strength. Resilience. A legacy?

Listen, listen to our stories and learn.
Wisdom, a sacred urn.
Our tales. The past survives.
Our dreams. Our futures thrive.

Antje Bothin
Nighttime

Experiences of bright nights
Loud and scary
Danger in the air
Children fully awake

Another noise
Far away
Bringing death
To poor souls

Fire in the skies
Will it ever end?
Mankind doesn't learn
From past mistakes
Memories of dark nights
Peaceful and clear
Moths in the air and
Families sleeping

Yasmin S Brown
what is africa

what is africa
if not a deep reflection
                    expressed by african americans
                    as
a loaded question
of history
                    we want to explore
but a continent that is much more
than a place will ever understand

how we envisioned
such beautiful land with rainforests and exotic safaris
can provide human cages
alongside rolling bodies of water
displayed cargo taken to a stolen land

an auction place for colonizers
to pick and trade my ancestors
for food and weapons
bargain and taken away
to a non-sovereign migration

a land where they were no longer a person
but property to the rich elite nation
enslaved
like a can of sardines
packed away below deck
then whisked away   it was obscene

chained together   never to be seen again
ill and murdered   dumped overboard
washed away as if they never existed

they did exist!

i am living proof
with dna from cameroon
congo and western bantu
even benin and togo
ivory coast

ghana
nigeria
and mali
a labelled african american researching her birth

unfortunately, they are unable to see the progress
of solidarity and independence   liberation
into a democracy
fighting for peace and sovereignty
to bring unity
liberation with a vision of prosperity
building bridges   of harmonized displays
                of humanitarian freedom
for the people, by the people

Yasmin S Brown
Strategic Unification

Gliding through the air
Like a blow from Cassius Clay
Unleashing displacement
Like an African refugee migration

Forced to travel
In the 17th and 19th century
Forced to build an economy and industry

Cotton and Textile
America's oppression with authority
A more permanent migration
Economic risk-taking

Converting
Name changes
Like Muhammad Ali
Drafted into a war so we can be free
To show stability and security

Transcending into a future with integrity
Cascading love, peace and light
With an extension across the Atlantic Ocean
Where we once used to be

Carrying memories moving forward
Through experience and education
In the words of Nelson Mandela,
"Education is the most powerful weapon
"Which you can use to change the world"
Throughout African and American nations

M. Chambers
African Origins

In the morning of the world,
I walked out of Africa.
Carrying a basket,
the seeds of History.
Sowed them in Kemet,
Black land of the Pharaohs;
brought them to Babylon, to Greece and to Rome.
Septimus Severus,
Proud Libyan Emperor.
Augustine the Saint,
African-born.

Tracing the mortar lines
in Great Zimbabwe.
Echoing on the ruins
of forest-bound Gedi.
Weeping at wall-torn Benin,
and the scars,
where there should be faces.
Hearing a condemnation
from Mansa Musa, on his throne of gold.

Sighing across the desert
on the dreams of Tuareg riders,
to sun-dark tombs, redolent with memories.
Those dreams,
Those memories,
sold in markets,
trampled in the fields of profit.
Where we gave you music,
out of the ghettoes of despair.

Now,
do you come
at the end of all journeys,
saying our nations are "developing"?
Daring to tell me
what freedom means?
I answer from the world's early morning.
I have been with you through all the migrations,

contributing silently
to all you became.

You don't know me.
You have never known me.
You don't even know yourselves.

M. Chambers
African Exile
An African statue in my collection, once a fertility statue of the Fang people

Dragged from her home.
Shipped like a commodity,
put up for sale,
auctioned off as property.
Passed from hand to hand.
Always a temporary place.

Shadows on the glittering eyes.
Sun warming palm-oiled surfaces.
Tender care of years,
Lustre of love.

Now she stands on the edge of my table.
Solemn statue,
frozen in the act of remembering.
Eyes looking through walls
at scenes of lost innocence.
Joyous songs of community
lacing the paths.
Flower-laughs of children,
planted along the way.
A canopy of dancers weaving histories.
Stories of Anansi,
and the kings of old.

There, in the still evening,
forest voices flow.
The barking cry of Mokele Mbembe,
mingling with the crackling fires.
A chorus of creatures in the softer darkness.
From far away,
The reassuring hornbill.
Singing her home.

Barrington Gordon
No Buts… (Universal Declaration of Human Rights?)

1. *"All human beings are born free and equal in dignity and rights…"* But some, based on our history, are more free and more equal than others. The elephant in the room rails, but the powers that be have ears full of human wax.

2. *"Everyone is entitled to all the rights and freedoms set forth in this Declaration…"* But here we are, war after war reported, and still puzzling over who gets what. Maslow would turn in his grave. Food, water, shelter and clothing are at a premium, paid for through an abundance of continuous, accepted suffering.

3. *"Everyone has the right to life, liberty and security of a person…"* But we watch in real-time as our environments are torn apart, and money, with its tentacles/ed sisters and brothers, profit and gain, reaches out with barbed fingers but never joins the voices that complain.

4. *"No one shall be held in slavery or servitude; slavery and the slave trade shall be prohibited in all their forms…"* But so many are enslaved, in economic bondage, for the basics of life; others tell them who, when, where and how they are allowed to move, trade and exist. The spider's web tightens. Children are sold for their economic and sexual labour. A booming industry!

5. *"No one shall be subjected to torture or to cruel, inhuman or degrading treatment or punishment…"* Did you not hear what I said before?

6. *"Everyone has the right to recognition everywhere as a person before the law…"* But, why else would they be standing before the law?

7. *"All are equal before the law and are entitled without any discrimination to equal protection of the law…"* But the evidence, for too long, shows that this is clearly not the case.

8. *"Everyone has the right to an effective remedy by the competent national tribunals for acts violating the fundamental rights granted him by the constitution or by law…"* But can you give me back my land, inheritance, children, wife, parents, ancestors, hopes and dreams?

9. *"No one shall be subjected to arbitrary arrest, detention or exile…"* In humanity's name, I demand time served by Nelson, Bob, Sojourner and Nanny. Need I go on?

10. *"Everyone is entitled in full equality to a fair and public hearing by an independent and impartial tribunal, in the determination of his rights and obligations and of any criminal charge against him."* But, what about her?

11. *"Everyone charged with a penal offence has the right to be presumed innocent until proven guilty according to law in a public trial at which he has had all the guarantees necessary for his defence...'* But, how can I be charged when I did nothing wrong in the first place? We demand that this farcical conversation ends immediately. We demand that all rights and full membership to the human race are restored for all African peoples. We demand that all past, present and future benefits are restored and protected!

NO BUTS!

Zainab M. Hassan
A Dreadful Day

I got a call: "My nephew is missing.
"His boat left Libya for Italy's shore,
"but there is no sign of it."

My heart turned cold, "What boat?" I asked,
my mind in flight. "Why wasn't I told
"he was going to ride a boat? Had I known,
"I would have begged him
"to stay,
"not risk the tide."

Last call from my nephew started playing in my mind:
"*Eedo*[1] I got a line – a travel deal, you see.
"From Cairo to Libya, then to Europe. Just send some money,
"I will do the rest."

I said: "No problem, my nephew."
So many times, like a broken recorder,
my brain kept replaying his words: "Eedo I got a line.
"Eedo I got a deal."

If only I knew.
The deal was with smugglers
A line to an overcrowded boat,
sailing into tidal waves high and deadly.

If only I knew.
This deal I paid for would lead you nowhere.
It would be a line to my lifelong guilt.

If only I could see you.

If only I could know your fate.

If only you could know my pain.

---

[1]*Eedo*: aunt.

If only the sea could speak and share.
Stories and secrets of *tahriib*[2]
Lost in waves of despair.

If only the pregnant sea could deliver.
You, your boat, and your companions.
After 22 years, by any chance,
ARE YOU ALIVE?

After that dreadful day when we learned of your loss,
In the middle of so many nights, I write to tame the pain.
The war, the loss,

the pain won't end.

Yet poems come like falling rain.
They fill my nights and haunt my day
Words that won't just fade away.
Words ...

---

[2] *Tahriib*: An Arabic word meaning smuggling which has been adopted into the Somali language and is mainly associated with illicit migration and activities such as smuggling and human trafficking.

Zainab M. Hassan
Breath of Identity

Black. Woman. Somali. Muslim. African. Immigrant. Black American.
Woman of Color. Somali American. Somali diaspora. Muslim American.
Muslim Immigrant. African-Immigrant. African American. African
diaspora.

Pan-African. Philanthropist.   I can breathe.

Profiling. Racism. Islamophobia
Discrimination. Injustice.
17 lives. 17 traits. 17 identities.
17 antiracism-fueling oxygen tanks.   I can breathe.

Can't be seen
        The wind.
Moving at the speed of light.
A cyclone engulfing.   I can breathe.

Can't lay your hands on me
        A fire.
Flames ablaze.
Hot volcanic eruption.   I can breathe.

Can't put your knee on my neck
        A fluid.
Water flowing with motion.
Dispersing into freedom.   I can breathe.

Can't hear me
        A light.
Shining sunlight.
Stars of the heavenly bodies.   I can breathe.

Can't be moved or removed
        The earth.
Grounded in soil.
Firmly anchored.   I can breathe.

Can't be bunched or beaten
        A rock.
Strong and firm.

Pillar of unwavering strength.   I can breathe.
Humbleness and kindness
        Humanity.
Love and peace embodied.
A catalyst for change.   I can breathe.

Rooted and centered
        Resilient.
African immigrant woman.
With ease and graceful strength.   I can breathe.

Zita Holbourne
Back To Where You Came From

Go back to where you came from they said
The thought of how I could do this went round in my head
I closed my eyes and thought about it for a while
Back to East London where I lived
Back to Peckham where I grew up
Back to Camberwell where I was born
Back to my mother's womb where I first started life
Back to my roots, but what were they?
Were they the island of Trinidad where my mother grew up
South London where my father was raised
The rolling hills of Wales, Rhondda Valley,
where my great grandfather migrated from
Or an unknown part of West Africa
where my mother's ancestors were taken and transported
In inhumane conditions, enslaved on plantations?

So many choices, South London, Wales, Trinidad, West Africa

Unable to settle on which location the angry man before me meant
I turned to his snarling–mouthed, rank–breathed, rotten–toothed, red face
And asked him: go back to where I came from when?
Yesterday, as a child, when I was born or were you referring
to my multi-heritage roots spanning three continents, multiple countries
and several centuries?

Trying to be smart are yah? He snarled
Smarter than you could or will ever be, I replied politely.
I bade him farewell, wishing him a good day
Before I walked away and went back to where I came from – a hotel in
Leeds.

Ugwuja Emmanuel Ifeanyichukwu
Reaped Dreams

We could not tell the difference
between "Japa" and being "Japa-ed"
– a steamed vomit of the home that *bred* us,
or a discarded guinea pig
to a foreign land that *dread* us.
We journeyed through the black heart of Sahara,
dried up like *live & laugh* stock,
sending letters from Libya
inked with our raped identities,
reaped dreams,
ruptured destinies,
rotting seeds.
Even the blessed were stolen–
by ambition,
by greed,
by the hunger of dreams,
by anger,
by desire
to cultivate notes of paper.
Blinded by the mirage of oil wealth,
we longed for a bite
of their burger of life,
those dream–lives
we had always wanted.
And so,
the sea eats
our best grains.

Zan V. Johns
Covered by Prayer

When darkness looms, I retreat within my soul.
I am brave because I know what covers me—
I'm covered by the prayers of my ancestors
Prayers from Africa's Republic of Cameroon
Prayers from the bottom of the ships—
vessels that drowned dreams and freedom
in the deepest darkest depths of the ocean.
I'm covered by their incessant prayers for survival
and their woeful prayers for home.
I am covered by the prayers of strong tortured men—
the men who landed in darkness—tormented
Prayers that cleansed their soiled battered bodies
Prayers that replenished their broken spirits
Prayers that relinquished their royalty
Prayers that preserved their regal essence
Prayers that calmed unspeakable anguish
Prayers that caused them to love despite peril
I follow the light of my resilient people
who prayed for me through centuries of hell
I'm covered by the prayers that brought us through
Prayers that buoyed us to rise above
Prayers that protect me when the outside looms dark.

Nandi Jola
nostalgia

you say your mother is not a racist   she is just from a certain era   when it
was ok to use 'them words'   you say this as you invite me over for dinner
I don't know how to explain my dilemma to you   that the era you are talking
about   was the most violent   most racist and most segregated   that was
probably when Apartheid   Jim Crow laws and Empire were ruling   that is
what you call an era   so   to not have our conversation mixed up   because
your nostalgia and mine are two different things   if you remember the
Beatles   I remember Emmett Till

Nandi Jola
Black Women

If we were to honour Black women | what would we do | write an ode | an
obituary| an elegy | here lies all the women | who led the nations | now they
lay bare | their suffering spanned decades | endured humanity | Mary
Maynard Daly | who went into space | at the grind for the dime | until the
nickel erased her face | from history | they all came up Mississippi | singing
blues and jazz | carried a smile | on their faces | Harriet Tubman | on the
underground rail | kept going back | Augusta Savage | painted history | they
raised us on their backs | they sang a melody | a lullaby to keep the peace |
for peace's sake | royalty is your name | regal you are | you righteous heirs |
Queens | the white house on the hill was built by your bare hands | rise.

Samuel Julius Habakkuk Kargbo
Victim of Tribalism

In the heart of Sierra Leone's diamond land
Footprints of tribalism and the cruel hands of nepotism
Ravage my country's light. The Pursuit of Education
Was once an honourable thing, but today the system
Comprises men and women fighting tribal wars

A victim of circumstance, I dared to dream
But tribal biases almost sunk my youthful gleam
The rats and bats tried to deny my worth
Held by man's contempt, I resolved to seek avenues
Beyond the pain, far from my motherland

Teaching became my solace, my pullout path
But it did not bring gold to the table
Patriots in front of the cameras but serpents in nature
Scarcity of good jobs, afraid to seek knowledge here
Cyprus beckoned, pledging a new stage

Portents of the tentacles of tribalism
I borrowed funds, sought loans and family aid
To flee the organized shackles of a mildewed system
Pay-offs, holes, and teaching defects profound
A damaged system where merit is seldom found

Towards Europe's coasts, aspiring for more
No laments as I voyaged, leaving behind bigotry
To secure a future, my expedition is not over
My ambitions soar high like the Rüppell's griffon vulture
Towards lands where education is free of hate

UK and America, with gestures of open arms
To foster aspirations amid life's infinite storms
In lands free from high, tribal, clouding waves
I see my dreams unwind beyond my shores
Like a priceless pearl, like the bluish sky

To shine, to conquer, to sculpt my fate
To grow, to contribute, to make a name
Education's beacon is a guiding star
Seeking better education, a pilgrimage of hope
Seeking an aura free of politics and chauvinism

I am far away from home; the hunt for progress
With new strands of trials, I valiantly cope
Full of life, it brings peace and rich hope
In the quest for knowledge lies true liberation
Victim of tribalism, echoes of freedom and justice

Samuel Julius Habakkuk Kargbo
Ramshackle Boats

In ramshackle boats, we steer the waves, Africans seeking fortune,
as we leave our caves our journey is full of perils, yet we sail
with high hopes of slaying our giants
motivated by dreams that refuse to crash

Through harsh, eating deserts and oceans deep
we journey on. No time to waste, no time to sleep,
desiring a land where prospects can be seized
where our aspirations can chuckle and smile
we seek a place where our labours can pay off

It is not just poverty that paddles our flight
but the security of a better, brighter light
where odd jobs pay more than office chairs
and living standards are like the rich in Africa
our hearts are heavy, our eyes are red

The West and even Africans marked us as illogical
but we are rational as we weigh our options
like a bald eagle before going after its prey
After two centuries of migration, our path is clearer
America, Europe, or where there is a clean shore

Just as the youth move, the elderly are part of the race
Driven by a desire to thrive and succeed
we navigate dangers and monsters to meet our needs
Many birds are flying. not just the poorest set sail
but those who decline to stop dreaming

Africa is beautiful, natural, and rich
but we are being blocked politically from reaching
our prize by the biased systems packed in layers
We know death snores close by, but we prefer
to take our chances in rubber rafts and fishing vessels

Temple run, coffins in water
Reaching there is all that matters
We are prepared for the deadly hallows
We believe once we reach the bounty
the fields we bloom, despair will leave the room

Another story of Africans' migration
One we love, one that has changed many lives
Our courage, our struggles, our universe
In ramshackle boats, we sail the unknown seas
in search of a life that brings butterflies

Anton Krueger
you're always going

you're always going, moving to the next event –
you're in an uber, bus or train, heading to catch a flight,
time hurls you onwards, you can never turn around.
you can never go back...

if you're reading this, you're unlikely to be homeless,
hard to relax on the run, few pages turn sleeping rough, or
when waiting for the truck with strange water from strangers...

so, you may not be one of the millions traversing the earth
searching for roof, refuge, relief; your village hasn't been burnt;
your children aren't hungry, no dust on your shoes –
it's more likely you're reading this on your ride to the airport,
windows up and aircon on, smooth electronica pulsing...

maybe you're catching a flight to beijing,
ticket on your phone for that metal bird
to carry you over the deserts and unfathomable seas
to that faraway continent to present
a brief paper to a roomful of scholars...
so you're coasting along at just the right temperature,
looking forward to your first bloody mary and
720 channels of on-board entertainment...

alongside the sleek east cape highway, game farms stretch out –
here and there a complicated wood stone entrances a luxury lodge.

you wonder what lies deeper, away from the national roads,
you remember the time you lost your way shortcutting to east london
when you faltered onto raw poverty, discovered dusty settlements,
deep dongas carved out of dirt, wide-eyed villagers surprised to see a car,
one tap for twenty households – they're not going anywhere.

you're always going, moving to the next event –
you're in an uber, bus or train, heading to catch a flight,
time hurls you onwards, you can never turn around.
you can never go back...

Thulani Mahlangu
from here to there

i used to think life was a fairytale,
till i was told about a fairy
in one of my tales
who was not short,
who did not have magical powers,
but was a creature who lived in our mist
who was hellbent on destroying my home

but i found that out too late.

i was taken away from my homeland,
because my home was no longer part of my land.
i need an escape plan,
so i pack my bags
make my way south to reach a place
that has democracy
a place i only heard of in my dreams
a place called south africa
where i can realize my own dream.

after some weeks of traveling,
ducking and diving from faces which are troubling
i land at a place called the city of gold
but where i was, only poverty ruled,
a place called hillbrow –
and i realized i cannot push any more.
then i became what the city was,
broken, a shadow of my former self.

selling packs of crack
any chance i get
just to cover the rent
put the rest in the stash
because i need to go to school one day
and see myself given another chance
to make it good. so,
from here to there i move,
make my way to a better life.
that is all i need
to continue living this life of mine.

Thulani Mahlangu
Where I Am From

I am from Mamelodi,
Where funerals are louder than the churches,
Where children learn to dodge grief
Before they learn to cross streets.
Here, danger is a neighbor,
But so is resilience;
We sing louder, we laugh sharper,
We love as if tomorrow is already mourning.

My grandparents are shadows in photographs,
Their names stitched in whispers.
I hardly knew their faces,
Yet I carry their absence like inheritance.
Migration is the ghost story of my blood
Not told, but felt in the way my mother moves houses
Like prayers,
In the way my father never unpacks fully.

Through my lineage
We have lived in rooms that remembered our hunger,
Flats that smelled of paraffin and Sundays,
Streets that taught us
That mobility is not only about leaving,
But about surviving the same place every day.

I know nothing of my ancestors' first steps,
So I write them into being:
I imagine them barefoot,
Naming rivers after children not yet born,
Singing Ndebele hymns against the wind.

I speak in many tongues:
Ndebele, Zulu, English,
A little Xhosa, Pedi, Spanish.
Each language is a door,
Some I was born inside,
Some I had to knock at.
In Ndebele we tell stories of men who walk far
And return as cattle herders or bones.
In Zulu the idioms stampede like warriors,

In Xhosa the rhythm is rain,
In English the tongue becomes paper,
In Spanish I stumble, but I dream.

Africa is not a question mark to me,
It is an exclamation!
It is dust on my shoes,
Braids in my sister's hands,
A beat on my laptop at midnight.
Being African is carrying many homes
In a single chest,
Knowing my laughter can echo in Lagos,
My tears can salt Cape Town,
My poem can live in Cairo.

In 2063 I see Africa standing tall,
Not begging, not waiting,
But singing in its own orchestra of nations.
I see artists shaping parliaments,
I see children learning our languages first,
I see us trading in stories,
Not only in gold.
And I, LaShawn,
Son of Mamelodi's restless ground,
Will have a hand in that tomorrow,
Not just for Africa,
But for a world that once forgot her name.

Esther Mamadou
Más que la luna al sol[1]

Ansou is a fisherman and knows how to swim.
The only one on the flimsy boat who knows how to swim
And still he only sees the terror of the night
Moussa, by his side, is only 15 years old
He is brave, although he does not stop shaking in the cold
He can only see within the multitude of waves
The demons of the afterlife coming for his soul
Another two days left
Spain or Death
Barça wala Barskh
Dawn rises
A sunrise in the horizon
Moon and Sun showing up for life
Dancing together, illuminating their path.

---

[1] *Más que la luna al sol* translates to "More than the moon to the sun".
    Since 2014, 3986 Africans have perished in the Atlantic migration route to the Canary Islands. Used by thousands of migrants since at least 1994, deaths have been recorded each year since 1999 by journalists, advocacy groups, and, since 2014, by the Missing Migrants Project. The route to the Canary Islands is extremely hazardous due in large part to the length of the overseas journey and lack of dedicated search-and-rescue capacity. <https://missingmigrants.iom.int/region/mediterranean> [accessed: 5 November 2025]

Monica Manolachi
Grace on the move

This poem is about grace.
It has no childhood.
It has come from far away,
crossing the desert.
It is living on wild fruits.
Although hardly visible,
I have found it at the borders.
It is tired and hurt.
It has no colour, no smell.
It is crying, but who can hear it?
It seems lost, but it is not lost.
It has lost trust and
is searching for it all around.
It has no papers, no debts.
I am trying to touch it,
but it steps back in fear.
I am not doing anything for a while.
I am leaving and it follows me.
Grace has no shadow.
I make room for it in the house.
We talk in our invented language.
There are many questions.
It is torn between me
and its place of origin.
When I wake up, I am surprised
to find it on my shoulder.
One day we go to the mountains.
On the train, grace asks:
What do you want from me?
Nothing special, I say.
We go up the slope
and it becomes very small,
disappearing among the clouds.
I know it is there.
I am a bit sad, almost crying.
I look at the wild fruits.
I am so hungry.

Monica Manolachi
Delivery Service

I see a boy stooped on his scooter
at the traffic light, head bowed,
attentive to the messages
on his smartphone, clean shoes
and hands gripping the handlebars.
He carries a red insulated bag
on his back, resting one foot
on the grey pavement, cautious
of the traffic hustle and bustle,
thinking of his clients.
The sun sets fire to the streets
of Bucharest, car horns blare
on the tree-lined boulevards
and it is a warm morning,
almost like in Senegal.
The boy takes a deep breath
and revs up before heading off
to his next destination with
menus, toys, medicines, flowers etc.
Here's your order, *mon ami*,
thank you, he says when
the customer opens the door.
A *mon ami* and a big smile
at every opened door.
His pay per day is less than
tourists spend on renting hookahs
with two rounds of flavours
and coals in the restaurants
of the Old Town.
Down in the cool, I wait
for the metro to come,
listening to Jerusalema
on my headphones
and making notes in my head
for a poem about the rider
at the traffic light.

Leonora Masini
To Lina

She is her lands
Her ancestors
Her mountains and sea

She is Eritrea and Sudan and Italy
A female shaped constellation that we stare at
In wonder

Her name means "net"
"palm tree" "delicate"
"tender" "truthful"
"rope" – a song from another time invades my ears –
L'inarrestabile, the unstoppable

She returned to Eritrea
To take her mother to Italy
And meet her father's family in Carrara

The net she launched in the sea
Returned full of memories from those dirty waters
The colony was the first one of the Kingdom of that Italy
We want to forget

Mama Lucia met the Italian side of the family
In a hug across time and space and colonial eras
But pain–
Less was her voice when she said
"I remember"

And as she remembered, Lina reminded us
Of the unbreakable bond of blood
And bones
Joining Italy and Eritrea
A history long forgotten,
They call it collective amnesia
For there are cowards

The unstoppable power of human ties
Return and reoccur
It is useless to try to break them

For a "palm tree" or a "net"
A "delicate" "tender" "truthful"
"rope"
Will always
spring out of history
to call for justice.

Leonora Masini
Only Berberè?

Traveling to Asmara from Rome
My mother and I
Do not know what to expect but the spicy fragrance she grew up with
Our neighbor Signora Elena, my mother recalls, used to cook Zighinì
"I learnt the recipe from my old friend Saba" Elena said
"Arrived in Italy after the War from Asmara, Eritrea
The first Italian colony"
– A spiced scent infuses my mother's memory

– Cardamom, cumin
Who are we?
Cinnamon, ginger, turmeric
Where do we come from?
Ajowan, coriander, pepper
Who are our people?
Is it only Berberè?
We do not remember it
Yet

Landed in Asmara
My mother and I
Follow the scent of Berberè
Wondering through the city together and remembering why
There are Cinema Impero and Cinema Roma
Il Corso, Il Caffè
And we are reminded of Askari and also Zaptiè

Cardamom, cumin
Who are we?
Cinnamon, ginger, turmeric
Where do we come from?
Ajowan, coriander, pepper
Who are our people?
Is it only Berberè?
We do not remember it
Yet

Leaving Asmara for Rome
My mother and I
Follow the scent of Berberè

44

Back to signora Elena's house together knowing why
There are myths of "the good colonizer"
And "missionaries' extraordinary lives"
Stolen treasures
Occupied lands
And the Italian Fascist War criminal Graziani Viceré

Cardamom, cumin
Who are we?
Cinnamon, ginger, turmeric
Where do we come from?
Ajowan, coriander, pepper
Who are our people?
Is it only Berberè? We do not remember it
Yet,

Italy occupied and consumed the landscape and resources of Eritrea for decades, from 1890 to 1941. The impoverishment of Eritreans and Eritrea, the political instability lasted decades after the end of Italian colonialism, and the contemporary forced migration that Eritrean people are suffering are legacies of the country's long history of colonial oppression.

My two poems, *To Lina* and *Only Berberè?* address the colonial past by focusing on images, voices, and memories of Eritreans living in Italy, or meeting Italians, and describing their memories of life under colonial occupation, memories that have been shared from their ancestors. The poems combine different temporalities – past, present, and future – to mirror the complexity of the trauma caused by colonial rules, which is a layered and long-lasting wound.

Several scholarly historical reconstructions addressing the topics of collective trauma and amnesia use sources stored in Italian archives and written in Italian by Italians; Eritrean sources are often left out. With this in mind, in my two poems I shift the focus to the Eritreans, their memories, voices, and storytelling.

These poems are based on true stories; the three women I mention, Lina, Saba and Lucia are Eritreans who migrated to the US and Sudan. I have met Lina and Saba in the US and in Italy; in the case of Lucia, I have been told the story of her life during Italian colonial rule by her family members. I choose women's memories and stories as the cores of my poems in the attempt to counterbalance the dominant male-centered literature and films about Eritrea and Eritreans produced during the colonial years by Italians.

Octavia McBride-Ahebee
Preparations for the Voyage to Lampedusa

I tagged him
like a suitcase
in our wedding henna and the indigo of our gods
so sand and salt water could not erase him,
using a hand-rolled cone of discarded plastic
I labeled him in Arabic on his forehead
with the translated love poems of Rumi
riding across the arch of each eyebrow,
I braided his eyelashes into a wind rose
to inform a faltering will where grace blew the hardest,
I pierced his ears
with Voltaire's call to give ourselves the gift
of living well,
on the palms of his hands, I rendered in sloppy English
the poetry of Lorde and Knight,
between the nervous Dogon masks that dressed his breasts
and the hairy lotus flowers
that framed a navel I love to get lost in
I sung in the double swirl of earth's only colors
a plea in Italian to be kind,
amid the spiraling canals of Sundiata's praise song
that ran up and down his legs, front and back,
I marked the empty spaces with the tattooed kisses
of his children and a p.o. box leading back to Kolokani,
on his stained fingernails I wrote our love dreams
– a quartered-filled belly of lamb and hibiscus,
a muted chest, feces that is thick
and whole and free of the world's disdain,
a means of stretching our children with ideas –
I wrote this is Bambara because it glows in the dark,
because it can lift a diminishing resolve from clutches
of a cold night desert,
disguised as a lullaby,
it can even dance on death's imminent arrival,
in the middle of a beautiful sea that will reject him,
that will remind him at the moment he is embraced
in a wet, frothy death hug
that this failure is not his,
it is not his.

Octavia McBride-Ahebee
1822/2014

Have you forgotten me
that Charleston girl
wrapped in a re-imagined rice sack
standing in an angel oak soaking in moss
watching through the swamp's own mourning
them hang our Demark
with no prayer or coin to take him over

kingfishers, flycatchers, delirious with lost
conspirators like me in Vesey's scheme of flight
chaperoned my exit from you
bound to an island of Providence   – Liberia
mean with fevers and stakes already claimed

it is me, your daughter, pushed through centuries of trial
lying here in a wrapper I used to dance in
to let fall when I climbed a lover
to let shield me against the wanted advances
of the harmattan and the rainy season

I am lying here at the foot of a baobab
older than what we share
lying here with a plague and my own daughter
on the magnanimous back of the earth
waiting for you to harvest your memory
to recognize the long-legged girl
on the arms of that Charleston oak
looking at what we used to be

Karuna Mistry
The Isthmus That Splits Us

by bare feet we move through
territory, wilderness and harsh terrain
carrying children on our backs, weapons
and possessions in hand   propelled
by survival's obsession

the isthmus that splits two lands
allows us to spill our contents onto new continent
free to roam and leave old roots   to rest
in the arid, red soils behind

we hunt, forage, kill
salvage, use, and upskill
survival depends on wit
and wit depends on will

we care for the injured and weak
carry you in our women   – their wombs
warmly house the unmade words
that we may scatter into the world

we are dependent   as your descendants,
Africanus, we live through you

Karuna Mistry
Perspectives (Home from Home)

I.

A house is not a home – just brick as its bone
No TV or computer; barely any furniture

Mould in the bathroom, dust in the bedroom
Replace the wallpaper with last month's newspaper

Staring at blank walls when no one calls
Pay as you go – paying top-up too slow

Not a soul in the house except for a mouse
When nobody's around to hear a living sound

Switch the central heating or pay for eating?
                – Decide
Make ends meet in this filthy old street
                – Suicide?

II.

Try to be hopeful and not give up when life is proving more than tough
Meant to search the meaning of life when life is not filled with strife

Find me some upliftment; grant me that fulfilment
Back home, friends and family made for a community

Meals were certainly better when people ate together
Here, to lift one's spirit is by no means an easy ticket

Different weather, cuisine and culture
But a new life to find by shifting my mind

Overcome my nerve and selflessly serve
                – Society
Do not expect and perhaps earn respect
                – Dignity?

Jenny Mitchell
Country Marks

The cabbie's face is scarred,
three scores on either cheek,
pale paths cut into brown.

My friends, both white,
turn pink to see me point,
but he is keen to speak.

These are my country marks.
Yoruba signs so we can meet
if scattered wide. I'm known

as Adebayo, meaning Crown
has met with Joy. My land
is east Benin, and you?

I say north London but he laughs:
You have no home. You're lost.
So many here are born of slaves.

My people are to blame.
We should have killed the whites
who chained your people in a hold.

My friends begin to squirm,
but I stare as he cries out loud,
forehead on the steering wheel.

I slap his shoulder to avoid a crash.
He will not take the fare, calls me
Sister, wishing *Peace and Love.*

Jenny Mitchell
Looking at the Benin Bronzes

What are you doing here?
What are you saying that I cannot hear?
Move more. Move your lips more.
I want you to show me your words.

Your words are watching me.
I see you smiling distrust
Distrust.

I will not move till you open
Your mouth.

Grow your mouth.
Say what I want you to hear.

I am here and you hear me I'm sure
With your crown,
No, your heart.

I step back
To take you all in,
So much age in the shine of your skin

You are smiling
Your eyes.
But above me a flag,

And behind you those flowers and leaves.
Those flowers and leaves are so wild,
They would want you to speak.

But your eyes are too old
With distrust,
More distrust.

A church in the shape of your head.

Words are alive,
Let them speak.

Nasra Dahir Mohamed
I Am Somali

They say, Talk about migration.
I ask, Where do I start?
Didn't I own the whole world?
Aren't we all from Adam and Eve?
Aren't we all bound to die?
Which makes us all migrants.
I am connected wherever I go
Because I am human,
Believing we are all from one parent.
Unless you're that weird brother, sister or relative,
Who doesn't like siblings to stay for a while?
In that case, it's okay. I will migrate.

They ask how migration affected me.
I ask how it didn't affect me.
I am Somali, moving is in my blood –
A nomad. It's all I know.
Migrating from one place to another.
Once, I ran from drought,
Instead of changing my lifestyle.
Why would I? I ran from clan conflicts,
Instead of understanding the root cause.
Sometimes we fight just to prove we are warriors.
Don't ask why that's important.

I am Somali. Rooted in this land.
Though it's dry and dusty,
It's home to me.
Borders don't restrict me
Because I am a nomad.
Crossing borders
For my camel,
For a better life,
For better education,
To see the rest of the globe.

Wandering thoughts fill my head,
Wondering where I'd be instead.
Would I shine in other lands
Or is this path where I stand all that there is?

The world sees me.
Flaws and all.
In politics,
I sometimes fall.
Maybe my purpose is to roam, explore, and journey alone.

Nasra Dahir Mohamed
Why We Left

I came home in the evening, and my mother asked me to milk the goats and the sheep. I did it. Afterwards, we started playing around, singing the whole night. I was so happy that night because it was a full moon. My father arrived later and said we were moving to another place because, even though the place we were in was beautiful and was near mountains, there was no rain here. We couldn't find water for our livestock. At midnight, we started preparing our camels, putting our materials on them, and started traveling. I was with the goats and sheep. After traveling for a while, we heard a noise. It was huge. Our cows stopped moving. And our he-camel stopped and started looking around. It was as if he was ready to defend the rest of the camels and the family. I had never seen a lion before. I had only heard about them. But this time, there he was, right in front of me.

Mariam Mohammed
The B(lack)ody as a map to self

Something in this place resurrects dead bodies in my mind:

the prayer of my grandmother's granny sings in my heart &

leaves footprints of hope on my skin—

everyone who knew Grandma tells me tales of

how her eyes held onto something   too far away from her reach till

in them, a lone star shone on her deathbed.

Mama says my gait resembles that of a (wo)man

: not so much like a woman, less like a man

So, she spends so much time on her knees

& begs her God to fix the broken piece in me // I hold words

on my tongue like an egg—Mama has known no other way to live than to breathe.

The soil beneath my feet is a white one & it has taught me about my (s)kin. I rescue

ghosts & survive on their tears in my thirst for truth. (Desp)air fills my lungs &

leads me to the darkness, where I utter prayers in a language alien

to Mama's tongue. I hear the fear in her voice when she calls

& hears strange sounds in my throat. We say goodbyes

as she prays some more for me to find my way—

a lost sheep into the barn that raised me—

back to my roots—where I'm unsure

to call home—but I do not

belong (t)here.

Mariam Mohammed
From where do I come?

The sea may have swallowed more of my kind
than I can ever imagine. I heard—I am told—stories of
how my skin earned its name. If you trace the map on
my body to the land that swallowed the umbilical cord
of my ancestors, you may understand the energy in my gait
& understand the meaning of the tears in my eyes. If you
trace the scar on my left cheek to my roots, you may
understand why my being screams of survival.

My heart weeps at the thought of the Red sea
that connects my land to the Lord's.

Today, I met my sister in the waiting room.
She told me of her plans to take an ancestry test:
Well, after I asked her: from where do you come?
I saw my reflection in the pool of tears in her eyes.
She told me: if I just keep walking,
I might find my way.

Fauziyatu 'Fauzi' Moro
Echoes of A Migrant's Ritual

Many moons before roaring engines shuttled dreams between places
She journeyed down rivers with many familiar faces
At a stopover in Bamboi, somewhere between home and hope
She immortalized her identity, bound to her skin like a tightrope

Blisters,
Birthed from the stinging union of skin and cashew bark
Blisters,
Healing into rugged body art:
Bechemyel, her birth name
Weelo, her birthplace

Tomorrow when her once tight skin folds and her fraying memory
            barely holds
The skin map on her aged arm will be the identity charm
Offering the gentle trigger
Needed to retrace her steps upriver

Remind Mugwambani
Africa's Children

We are the sons and daughters of Africa's soil.
On our shoulders, we carry the past and the present.
In our eyes, we carry the future,
the weight of migration,
a struggle we can't deny.

We are the ones who crossed unnumbered borders, seas, and time zones
in search of hope, a better life,
a chance to shine.

We left behind the familiar, the known, and the dear.

We face the unknown.

On our treacherous march,
we encountered strangers.
Some met us with kindness,
others with hatred and evil
in their eyes and hearts.

We faced the brutality of borders,
the cruelty of fate.

Destiny gazed upon us and wept.
Yet, we persevered.
Our resilience, our greatest stronghold.

We soldier on,
carrying the scars of our past,
the memories of loved ones lost
back home
or in dangerous seas and rivers.
They were searching for a place to call home.
African nomads looking for green pastures.

Upon us is a grief that will last forever.

At night and during the day,
we dream

of a glorious,
brighter future,
a world where migration is a choice
not a desperate measure.

We are Africa's children,
proud and strong.

We will shape the future of our continent
with our stories,
our voices,
and our hearts.

We will make lasting change.

Remind Mugwambani
Footsteps of Our Ancestors

In the footsteps of our ancestors
We roam, seeking greener pastures,
Like the tortoise, we carry our shells,
Our cultures, identities, and stories to tell.

What is a nation, but a dream of unity?
A fleeting thought, a moment's clarity,
Like the wind, it blows, and then subsides,
Leaving us in the dust of our pride.

We migrate across Africa's borders,
Like the birds in the sky, following the seasons.
We ask why? Why do we leave our motherland?
What do we seek in foreign lands?

Is it freedom, or a different form of captivity?
When elephants fight, it is the grass that suffers,
But what of the grass that chooses to wander?
Is it not seeking new soil, new sunshine?

A new chance to grow, to flourish into its prime.
Like a mighty river, we flow. We twist and turn,
Carrying our memories, our hopes, our yearnings.

What lies ahead, what lies behind?
Is it not all the same, a journey of the mind?
What can be broken, but never held?
Is it not our hearts, our spirits, our stories untold?

What is a border, but a line in the sand?
Can it hold back the tide, the waves of our land?
We migrate, like the stars in the night,
Following our dreams, our guiding light.

Ambrose Musiyiwa
st georges walks into a pub

st georges,

does lynch mobs

reminds you
of strange fruit
swinging off southern trees?
strange fish
off small boats?

marine food?

fish n' chips,[1]
st georges?

a pint?

---

[1] In conversation with Helidah Ogude-Chambert. (2024). "Strange Fish", in *Japa Fire: An Anthology of Poems on African and African Diasporic Migration*. CivicLeicester, 2024: 72

Ambrose Musiyiwa
There Will Always Be One More Thing[1]

A nobleman, a man of God.
His name was George.
He confessed his belief
In the one true God.[2]

Patron Saint of Aragon, Catalonia, and England,
Patron Saint of Georgia, Germany and Greece,
Patron Saint of Lithuania, Moscow and Portugal,
Patron Saint of Romania, and Serbia,

His name was George.
He confessed his belief in the one true God.
A nobleman, a man of God, his name was George.

Somebody says[3] Europe can't cope
simply can't cope
with African and Asian refugees.[4]

We'd be over-run,
Patron Saint of Archers.

It'd be too much,
Patron Saint of Cavalry and Cavalrymen.

---

[1] In conversation with Toni Morrison who, in a 1975 speech, said: 'The function, the very serious function of racism is distraction. It keeps you from doing your work. It keeps you explaining, over and over again, your reason for being. Somebody says you have no language and you spend twenty years proving that you do. Somebody says your head isn't shaped properly so you have scientists working on the fact that it is. Somebody says you have no art, so you dredge that up. Somebody says you have no kingdoms, so you dredge that up. None of this is necessary. There will always be one more thing.' (Morrison, T. (1975). Lecture: A Humanist View. *The Black Agenda Review*, 26 March 2025. Available at: <https://www.blackagendareport.com/lecture-humanist-view-toni-morrison-1975> [accessed: 30 October 2025])

[2] Extract from The Georgslied (Song of St. George). Available at: <https://de.wikisource.org/wiki/Georgslied> [accessed: 30 October 2025]

[3] In conversation with Lady Blacksmith Mambazo. (1986). Homeless. Available at: <https://youtu.be/gfZxnVQHdgI?si=ZLYPHkqhMjRAx_us> [accessed: 30 October 2025]

[4] Krause, U. (2021). Colonial roots of the 1951 Refugee Convention and its effects on the global refugee regime. *J Int Relat Dev* 24, 599–626. Available at: <https://link.springer.com/article/10.1057/s41268-020-00205-9> [accessed: 30 October 2025]

We'd be ruined,
Patron Saint of Scouts and Soldiers.

We'd be overwhelmed,
Patron Saint of Riders and Saddlers.

We'd be tainted,
Patron Saint of Fencers and Field workers.

We'd be diluted

A noble man, a man of God.
His name was George.

Patron Saint of Ethiopia,
Lebanon,
Palestine,
and Syria,

Somebody says African and Asian men
women
and children
fleeing war
conflict
persecution
climate change
extreme poverty
violence

do so

illegally.

His name was George.
He confessed his belief in the one true God.
He was afflicted with many evils,
But his spirit was not broken.

Somebody says African and Asian refugees
men
women
and children
can't possibly be human

can only be illegal

criminal

for surviving border zones
deserts
seas
and the jungle,

can't be human

can only be small boats

for swimming the moat
and scaling the fortress,

can't be human

for wanting to feel safe
and for wanting to live
breathe
dream
flourish,
and prosper

simply

cannot

can't be human

He was afflicted with many evils,
But his spirit was not broken.
He confessed his belief in the one true God.

Patron Saint of Syria,
Palestine,
Lebanon,
and Ethiopia,

Somebody says Europe can't cope
simply can't cope
with this invasion

with these ~~black, Muslim~~ numbers

these small boats

these non-humans

can't possibly do for ~~Black~~ African and ~~Muslim~~ Asian refugees
what we did for ~~white, Christian, blue-eyed, blond, middle-class, working-class European men women and children~~ Ukrainian refugees ~~who look like us and live in houses and drive cars and go on holiday and go to work, church, the club, and school—like us—and who ...~~[5]

Then, when he had died,
He arose again from the dead.
He arose again from the dead.
And began at once to preach.

Patron Saint of Portugal, England, and Germany,
Patron Saint of Aragon, Catalonia, and Lithuania,
Patron Saint of Serbia, Romania, and Greece,
Patron Saint of Moscow and Georgia,

A noble man, a man of God.
His name was George.

Somebody says Europe is a garden
built of freedom
economic prosperity
and social cohesion[6]

an exception

---

[5] Limbong, A. 2022. "Why Ukrainians are being treated differently than refugees from other countries". *npr*, February 28. Available at: <https://www.npr.org/2022/02/28/1083580981/why-ukrainians-are-being-treated-differently-than-refugees-from-other-countries> [accessed: 8 November 2025]
[6] Borrell, J. (2022). European Diplomatic Academy: Opening remarks by High Representative Josep Borrell at the inauguration of the pilot programme. European Commission, 13 October. Available at: <https://www.eeas.europa.eu/eeas/european-diplomatic-academy-opening-remarks-high-representative-josep-borrell-inauguration-pilot_en> [accessed: 30 October 2025]

built of beautiful things
intellectual life
and wellbeing

Yes, we've built a garden.
Europe is a garden,
and the rest of the world, a jungle.[7]

Then, when he had died,
He arose again from the dead.
He arose again from the dead.
And began at once to preach.

Patron Saint of Moscow, Georgia, and Serbia,
Patron Saint of Romania, Lithuania, and Greece,
Patron Saint of Portugal, Aragon, and Catalonia,
Patron Saint of England, and Germany,

Somebody says the jungle
by different ways and means
will invade us[8]

He arose again from the dead.
He arose again from the dead
And began at once to preach.

Protector against the plague,
Protector against leprosy,
Protector against venomous snakes,

His name was George.
He confessed his belief in the one true God.
A nobleman, a man of God, his name was George.

Somebody says African and Asian men, women and children
drowning four times[9]
cannot be human
simply cannot,

---

[7] Borrell, J. (2022)

[8] *Ibid*

[9] Hayden, S. (2022). *My Fourth Time, We Drowned*. Fourth Estate, 2022

can't be human

can only be illegal
warehousable
transportable
trade-able
fungible
units
swarms
waves
a flood
mermen tripping on fantasies of walking on land sailing oceans on ship rudders[10]
Icarus[11] intent on disturbing 31-year-old, Clapham, south-west London software engineer's Polish beer[12]
manacled, straitjacketed birds[13] on chartered deportation flights ~~cattle trucks~~ still–bursting throttling songs of freedom[14] through manacled legs torn ligaments shattered spines   broken ~~wrist~~ings   broken necks   crushed chests   collapsed lungs[15]
nothing to see here   nothing to hear
would you like something to eat, ma'am
something to drink, sir
fasten your seatbelts
enjoy the onboard entertainment
one in, one out
deal

[10] Four Nigerians survive 14 days on ship's rudder before Brazilian rescue. *The Guardian*, 1 August 2023. Available at: <https://www.theguardian.com/world/2023/aug/01/four-nigerians-survive-ship-rudder-brazil-rescue> [accessed: 30 October 2025]
[11] In conversation with Amanda Holiday. (2024). "African Icarus", in *Japa Fire: An Anthology of Poems on African and African Diasporic Migration*. CivicLeicester, 2024: 32
[12] Kale, S. (2021). Out of thin air: the mystery of the man who fell from the sky. *The Guardian*, 15 April 2021. Available at: <https://www.theguardian.com/world/2021/apr/15/man-who-fell-from-the-sky-airplane-stowaway-kenya-london> [accessed: 30 October 2025]
[13] In conversation with Maya Angelou's "Cage Bird", on Poets Speak (2024). MAYA ANGELOU reads "Caged Bird". Available at: <https://youtu.be/ZwKsjTVhfcU?si=1M_wvfae-JmzP84R> [accessed: 30 October 2025]
[14] In conversation with Bob Marley and The Wailers (1991). Redemption Song. Available at: <https://www.youtube.com/watch?v=B0xceHDpHcc> [accessed: 30 October 2025]
[15] Deaths of immigration detainees. 2017-2025. Inquest. Available at: <https://www.inquest.org.uk/deaths-of-immigration-detainees> [accessed: 30 October 2025]

of single
fighting age
illegal
numbers, meeennn
with no rights
to want

our jobs,
our women
our schools
our social housing
our NHS
hotels
homes

children,
He arose again from the dead
And began at once to preach.

Patron Saint of Ethiopia,
Patron Saint of Lebanon,
Patron Saint of Syria,
Patron Saint of Palestine,

Somebody says Britain must
reduce the numbers
send the drones
send the jet skis, wave machines and floating walls
send the navy
send the army
send M
MI5
MI6
James Bond
the police
The Doctor
send Peppa
Pig
send the patriots, knights, and SAS
send the villagers and towners
send Rupert Paddington, and Winnie
Toad too
round up

clear out
by any means
stop ~~them~~ the invasion
bang ~~them~~ up
string ~~them~~ up
reduce
smash
the foreign~~ers~~ ~~the Africans~~ ~~the Muslims~~ small boats ~~numbers~~
send ~~them~~ back
carcasses
throw ~~them~~ back
against the border
the sewer
~~vermin~~
the river
the sea
human zoos
concentration camps
death camps
killing fields
weapons development & testing grounds
organ harvesting fields
~~fence them in~~
~~what I'd like to know is   would you push the button~~
open air & for-profit ~~prisons~~ containers
disused military barracks
offshore
out of sight
out of earshot
~~offshore rigs~~
~~prison ships~~ barges
~~prison colonies~~
~~shithole countries~~
Rwanda
Albania
Kosovo
fish and meat ~~markets~~ grinders
~~wars~~
let them drown
tents
sands
~~count them~~
~~monetise them~~

~~tag & track them~~
~~no rare earth minerals~~
~~nor oil and gas~~
~~nor semiconductors~~
~~nor markets for our missiles, bunker buster bombs and F-35s~~
these
~~biomass~~

O God,
who didst grant to Saint George strength and constancy,
preserve, through his intercession,
our faith from wavering[16]

because ~~for them~~
~~no visas~~
~~no e-gates~~
~~no family reunion~~
~~no safe routes~~
~~no sanctuary~~
~~because~~ they are not,
cannot be
can't be human

these numbers

these small boats
this invasion

~~cut their feet off~~
deflate ~~their~~ dinghies
the small boats
~~in the sun~~
~~let them drown~~
~~the Black African Muslim Asian carrion~~
~~in the night~~
detritus
~~in~~
~~at~~
~~within our~~
~~the border~~
driftwood

---

[16] Early church intercessory prayer

these

because we can't cope

because Europe is a garden

because the rest of the world
is ~~not blue-eyed blond~~ a jungle
and the jungle
wants

to invade
us.

He rose again from the dead.
He arose again from the dead
And began at once to preach.

And The Sirens, still —
with songs of freedom
— to thy treacherous coasts lure
the displaced

to these hard, hard coasts[17]

Wade in the water (we dey)
Wade in the water, children
Wade in the water (we dey)[18]

---

[17] In conversation with "Rule, Britannia!" (1763): 'The Muses, still with freedom found / Shall to thy happy coasts repair / Shall to thy happy, happy coasts repair / Blest isle regardless, with countless beauty places / And manly hearts to guard the fair'. Available at: <https://en.wikipedia.org/wiki/Rule,_Britannia!> [accessed: 30 October 2025]

[18] The Spirituals. (2021). Wade in the water. Available at <https://youtu.be/fxZ4H-gq_lc> [accessed: 30 October 2025]

Francis Muzofa
Old/Lonely/Homeless

I left like I was going to the shops
I thought it was just going to be two minutes four seconds
a typical sprinter's race

alas it became a marathon
a marathon on two fronts
a long illegal stay — foreigner
a long laborious shopping trip

ashes of grey hair
tell time with precision
for when I arrived
the grass on my head was blue black
now snow has invaded the black land

my energy levels didn't require energy drinks
my eyesight was flashlight
my muscles were cranes for hire
my brain was a huge processing plant
now it's totally a different me
a complete opposite of the former me

time has flown with all

I have nothing
no documents
no home
no family
no future
no wealth
no health
I am just a spent fly in a refrigerator
back home I am a villain
here I am just a sick dog in the neighbor's yard
the reason I left, has not been solved yet

should I fly to heaven?
should I just land here on earth?
if I die, will they bury me?
will my ancestors accept me?

Francis Muzofa
Serengeti Gazelles

Clamped in a vice
Pressured in a pressure cooker
Hammered into distraction

This is our reality
This is our tragedy
This is our reward
This is our award
Our inheritance for being born in Africa
Political destitutes
Economic slaves
Fatherless kids
Most Africans are
They bustle
They hustle
They tussle
In pain
All in vain

Many men perish at sea
They become shark relish at sea
Like tinned sardines they are packed in canoes
And paddled towards the darker greener grass
That Europe and America portray
Even the ocean is puzzled by the audacity
To attack the audacious ocean
With a mere canoe
Sadly only a couple make it to heaven.

Those who finally land
Live on borrowed land
They are not embraced by the system
They are embarrassed by the system
Their complexion and accent
Is their worst traitor
They have to constantly dodge immigration arrows
That are fired at every turn
To meet ends
Many hands are needed

At least four jobs have to be juggled
A kick in the loins
A blow to their health
They suffer both physically and emotionally
Such is the cursed lives of children of the jungle
Broken families
Broken cultures
Broken virtues
Broken dreams
Broken pockets
Broken lives
Self-esteem steamed out

Who is to blame
For the lame sheep
Is it our politicians
Is it our colonial masters
Is it our ignorance
Is it our arrogance
Is it our gods
Or our God

We are in a steel furnace
We are wood in a kiln
We are in hell where hailstorm rain
As the devils reign forks in hand

The economic graph is very skewed
The political abacus is one-sided
As the pride of lions grow and roar
The herd of gazelles are body and number thin
Fleas terrorize them
Fleeing from predators is routine
This is the fate of gazelles
In the Serengeti
Grief and Sorrow
Is their inherited surname and totem.

J.O. Neill
Complicity

He embodies his craft, the language of wood,
endowed like the grey of his seaglass eyes,
the flax of his caulk-flecked hair. It's unwise,
he has learned, to go against the grain; one should
plane along the path of least resistance. Good,
he says, palm flat to the yielding planks, tightening
up the maws of the clamps, while disguised by
his mind with its horde of further tasks, a mood
has been encroaching on his soul... They know,
the shipwrights, where the boats in the yard
are going, why they're building rows of shelves
into the hold. But their thoughts are in the crow's
nest. Though sleep wants no truck with facade:
packed into the slavers are themselves.

Jana van Niekerk
From God to Dust[1]

In our sleep, pain that cannot forget falls drop by drop upon the heart and in our despair, against our will comes wisdom through the awful grace of God.

Aeschylus: Agamemnon

I

Emergency years.
Haas Das se Nuuskas.[2]
More news at Seven, or as it happens.

God is in the dreadful things,
the small things,
the day they took all our furniture away.

It was time.

This house is a hundred years old.
And I have been congenitally unable to live.

I write in my little locker:
The Protest Poet,
running backwards and forewords
forwards and backwards
for words

and a poem for myself cannot be,
only that.

---

[1] Words attributed to Swami Venkatesananda, who visited District Six before it was demolished under Apartheid in South Africa in the 1960s. This poem was produced in response to a request for "A Protest Poem for the New South Africa"
[2] "News from the Bunny in a tie" – a popular children's programme in South Africa in the 1970s

II

The things we don't talk about.
Your Domestic and the Law.
Eating in front of hungry people.
oh god I am shrieking
top us gut us hang us out to dry!

The day Madam shat herself at the Beauty Counter
in Stuttafords
I tell you what,
the worst part was the smell,
sliding off gently.

When you don't believe that this is you,
When you don't believe
that this is mad
then Alice you have eaten me,
A shit sandwich,
A tin of fish's assholes
And camels have green teeth.

Who did this to you, then?

Old men in Polyester,
A Bint who should know better,
the fatty lip on lamb,
The Competition.

Huddled like bananas,
we can do no more.
Even my day is wearing a seatbelt.

(They) have hidden
burnt boiled broken
all your Play Stuff -

these children,
these angry children
they drive Jettas, Astras and Scenics now.

Toyota.
Cambrio.
Quite a ride.

I do not know myself,
I lay wasted by my subterfuge.

III

"Maybe we'll come to understand one another — "
this glorious existence,
a galaxy inside of me,
an Orchid,
and we wonder if there is a Love Palm on their toilet.

This is a house that people live in.

I am a Parvenu
I live on charity
I renounce my individuality.

And
in fact
everything passes.

Everything is change,
nothing has changed
the change bank,
the change lady,

it's all change,
it's been neglected for so long.

An Artemis,
always ready for the hunt,
hurt by accidental non-crimes —

This is an old house.

IV

And Peace, who is she?
The night of Divali
The festival of Luxmi,

it sounds like something from a dream.

— only if you feel
what's right in front of you —

paradise came to me like this poem did,
in daywear.

I looked up and saw it

light

The fallen angel
his perfect shattering
so that we should see
what colour we were made.

Dike Nwosu
A Journey Full Circle

It all started from the Biafran war.
Tribalism, Daddy didn't want none of it.
Fighting on the street and a whole lot worse.
Unseen forces hexed the people with a curse.

Biafra, Nigeria.
History, hysteria.
Problems in Africa, from Soweto to Liberia.
Daddy said no more.
A village chief switched to hustling.
And now he's London bound.

As the plane takes off,
He can hear the sounds of souls weeping and moaning.
Daddy knocks back shots of cognac,
Zoning,
Flying to destiny.
To leave his enemies behind.
As the mind tries to rewind.
He's looking forward,

Better days and times.
London and the goldmines.
The road was paved with gold, so Daddy heard.
Pound sterling to make, western world
Word.

Lonely London.
No blacks, no Irish and no dogs.
Throw in the towel, Enoch Powell.
Rivers of blood, skud.
Racial tensions,
But one love from the high-grade bud.
You like the taste, innit?

A mission, we got to begin it.
Aspirations to make it, win it.
Rise, we have to rise.
Though many of Babylon's traps,
They lay in wait,

Lay in disguise.
60s to 70s.
70s to 80s.
Daddy linked Mummy.
They had a couple babies.
At some stage, between a clean shave and a beard.
Many of his dreams and ambitions disappeared.
Hopes of being a doctor, lawyer, engineer.
Assimilate to hardship and economic fear.
Foreign soil,
Nine to five ain't much fun.
But love and lust when dad met mum.

He used to fetch water when he was in the village.
I grew up in concrete slums with sin spillage.
Go read your books, he said.

As the path of the indigenous ghetto youth ran red.
He projected his whole destiny onto his youths,
And told us we would know humans by their fruit.
In fact, he prophesied my whole path ahead.

It was my sister who phoned,
Told me my dad was dead.
Mummy's like Mary.
Daddy's like King Solomon.
Wisdom with too many ladies.
A bitter symphony as we work like clones.

When Daddy passed, we took the body home.

Back to the hood again.
Much tougher and wiser.
A miser with a pain disguiser.
Still, I'm a born riser.
To the crown through the Sephiroth path,
These are the Zion *hors d'oeuvres*.
Kinetic war stories swerve and curl,
To the Rasta man with deep talk
Of the pearl. My postcode missed me.
Know about my history.
Deep in street-thought
When the angels came and kissed me.

Dudes in jail, set them free, set sail.

Lost with the brethren.
The young black male.
Flight of the navigator.
Navigate your way home,
Through the paradox to the ancestors.

In God we believe,

As an evil spider weaves
A web mark of the beast
By which he deceives.

It's a warring zone,

Let's repatriate home.
No longer trapped like mind-controlled clones.
Full circle.

Dike Nwosu
not quite knowing our station

migration migration
is it joy and jubilation
or a space where
we are in limbo
not quite knowing our station?

     in the diaspora
          are we richer or poorer
          writing to articulate insight
          or just to record events
     trials and tribulations
          onwards and upwards
          through generations
     maybe we're going backwards
          when we analyse the state of the youth
yes we can
     learn a trade
     work
     or go to university and obtain degrees
yet still
     current trends
     suggest
     our youth are
feeling the heat
     in the street
dancing
          to a completely different beat
          death and destruction
     where confusion and callous crimewaves meet
     where postcodes clash
     gunshots
     knives
          stab
          slash
     regardless
          of friday prayers
          or sunday morning mass
     we are in trouble

a huge explosion

clear the rubble

migration migration
elevation
or toil and trouble

did I mention
that all the institutions are racist

did I mention
our boys are kicked out of school regularly
they can't all be footballers
a quota with not enough places
did I mention this

did I forget to mention that
we are stuck in a rat race
but we are not rats

we are a great people
scattered
battered
bruised
in captivity
with a story most captivating

we need to regain our greatness
and checkmate the checkmating

migration migration
is it joy and jubilation
or a space where
we are in limbo
not quite knowing our station?

Takunda G Nyika
Lamentations

He came into my dreams, my brother, crying.
He did, he disturbed my peaceful sleep, night.
He was sweating, but black-red drops, blood.
He told me, "Brother I'm back, from Jo'burg.
But I can no longer feel anything or see you.
They burned my skin with big n' black tyres.
I can no longer breath, here, see my windpipe.
Blunt, rusty machetes, my head, they cut it off.
Neither do I know or think anything is right.
My moon-white cerebrum gushed out, a fair.
Like a martyr, they threw stones, my head hurts.
Nor speak to you, that, I can no longer do that.
Taku young bro, don't sleep, lend me your ears.
Tell our mother not to cry for me, tell her that.
I will get the rest that the Lord promised, faith.
Don't tell her that I doubt for my place above.
For I die with a lump in my chest, too aching"
He looked at me with life-longing eyes, passion,
"All her life, our mother toiled, a mother bird.
I wished I could accumulate gold, but I didn't.
To rebuild her nest and in her aging rest, wish.
But noble I thought, a disgrace, a shame, I did.

"Tell our father nothing, but a warning, furore!
Lest he afflicts mom again, should I haunt him.
Tell our sister to choose another road, untaken.
Jo'burg isn't a dream place, but if, a nightmare.
Should they feed pigs with her breasts, I saw it.
I wish I could show my affection with materials.
But tell her my word, It's what I have, poor me.
And brother, listen closely, bow your head still.
I don't intend you to fill the blanks of my life, but
Always be around for mother, tell our sister too.
Kiki my unborn child, I wish I had seen her once.
Please do check up on her from birth to the age.
Tell her that her father was a good man indeed.
How much I wanted to gild our home, a castle.
Let her live royalty, all hail the Zezuru princess!
Blame my killers or what? Still a father I failed.
I shouldn't have gone Jo'burg, but another means.

"Tell my wife I love her as a tortoise loves its bark.
Tell my young wife to marry again, should she be.
I may be jealous, yes, but I won't be bitter, tell her
To try to forget me n' love the new man fully.
How much I hate infidelity even of the heart.
I won't even be bitter if as a mother she struggles
To cater for our daughter fully, let her know this.
I'll be with her as she faces all the odds, fair.
I'll intercede to God for her, I left a widow alone.

"My body lay bare n' black n' my breath, smoke.
In the foreign land, their air stinks hatred as hot.
I despise the land, come take my ashes home.
I die with bloody hatred for them, hot-red eyes.
And brother, do not avenge, remember our values.
I repeat, do not hate them brother, but be vigilant.
I fairly worked for bread, but see, unfairly dead."

Takunda G Nyika
Haunted

I strolled down Cowardice Crescent Street to the US
Screams like sirens of children in Soweto slammed my ears
"So where to? So where to? So where to? So where to?"
My head! The deafening shrill! I pressed my hands to ears
"Free Mandela yes; Freeze Mzansi not!" a repeated shrill

Abraham's divine voice from above thawed the screams
"Yes I am also the father of the fifty five nations!"
His name's sake followed like thunder and corn popping
"The Emancipation Proclamation transcends just slavery"
What! I ran back home baby—carrying the noisy wind

Darkness dethroned light, angry faces shone sideways
Nkrumah, Nyerere, Kenyatta, Mandela, Mugabe, Tshaka.
Selassie[1], Khama, Achebe, Sammory[2], Garvey and others
Mahatma Ghandi's and Mother Theresa's faces were sad
A Pharaoh mummy's forehead was written in blood, "Found and Lost"

Dark visions start fleeting all over my head, black and white
Images of a procession of negroes in chains into steam ships
Images of a thousand men with spears perishing to gun shots
Images of black women working with brooms wearing blue collars
Images of malnourished, big head, skinny black children wailing

Images of children crying, women sobbing and men running
While dark smoke, fire balls, fallen buildings, bullet shells
Hovering green helicopters, tankers, green trucks destroyed nature
Men in earth-camouflage and men marching punish my eyes
I threw myself to the ground; the images were a log to my eyes

"Fury at last! Fiery to last! Fury at last!" Martin Luther's distant call
Elands carrying beans with hot curry in the Caribbean islands
Rise from the seas with Toussaint and other saints as the riders
A note stained with blood with signatures of all great men stuck
In my hands, "We were freedom fighters, this is fear and doom infighting"

---

[1] Emperor Selassie of Ethiopia
[2] Sammory Toure a historical figure of West Africa

Joseph C Ogbonna
Don't Surprise Me Europe

I am Africa,
colonial Europe's partitioned cake

I am the ancestral habitat of the
itinerant welfare seeker,
the enslaved for the ephemeral promise
of Occidental and near Eastern Paradise

I am the fugitive or stateless,
from the battleweary enclave
and the audacious traveller
consumed by choppy sea conditions in his Odyssey
to fantasy and distant lands

I brave the blistering heat of the deserts
and the belligerent Maghreb
to have my needs sated in lands west of Bosporus

The corridors of death in the Sahara and central Mediterranean
are my routes to the grave,
there you will find my mass catacombs

But, don't surprise me Europe
with disdainful and squalid camps

Don't surprise me Europe
with pejorative and exploitative tasks

Don't surprise me Europe
with that age-old prejudice that enslaved me across the Atlantic

And don't surprise me Europe
with historic colonial and neocolonial stereotypes

Joseph C Ogbonna
Japa Quagmire

The skies hovering over Nigeria are gloomy,
to say the least. Terror groups proliferate
the two main axes
of the northern landscapes.
Shrinking opportunities,
bloated tariffs
and youth redundancy
plague its economic terrain.
Relegated to the very depths
are the eroded middle class
which Cossy belongs to.
Adding to his misery,
he hears about lucrative mining activities
in the terror belts of his beleaguered country.
He says, *I must Japa*[*].
But, by what means?
The perilous desert?
The dreary Mediterranean?
The elusive visa for an indigent African?
Oh, what a quagmire!

---

* *Japa*: a Yoruba expression that means 'run away', 'escape' or 'migrate'.

Tanure Ojaide
They Were Once Demigods

Only from so far away could I take them for what
they were not. I would have declared them gods
from a distance but fortunately I read and travel
and it takes living with them to really know them.

If I had not lived among them, how could I have
torn off the glorious mask that dressed them as heroes
instead of bands who hunted simple folks as animals!
How would I have known the depravity in their heads?

I live among them and know them closely. If one could meet
the hawk in its nest, one would discover its deprivations—
the famine it constantly suffers in the heavens, source of
human yearnings, to make it swoop to the earth for chickens!

It is not as told in the movies, Hollywood retouches—
the poor pathetic; the mass depressed citizenry
and capable of terrorism and worse things.
Lines of hungry folks snake round skyscrapers.

If I had not lived among them, I would have remained
fooled to invoke a god without a godhead.
I would have been a stranger to their world as they
had forced themselves as hosts in my homeland.

They have not yet cancelled the iniquities they rode
into knighthood and sainthood. History has all along
been a masquerade without a god as guardian of its charter.
It would take a lifetime of penitence to pay for the sacrilege.

I would not have known the hoax that history is.
I would not have seen through the theatrics
in proselytizing a godhead empty of truth.
I would not have known their true color.

Tanure Ojaide
Remembering Edinburgh, 1979

It pays not for a victim to be only angry, or
just forgive the unacknowledged unforgivable.
Should the victim burn down the abuser's home
or spit at the accursed face of the evil one?
I was not angry at the old woman in Edinburgh
who called me *Jimmy* to my face in the street.
I told her I am Tanure. "*Tanu* what?" she asked.
"Learn it, Miss Jim!" I shouted at her.
She dared not call me names again and later
"I like your name *Ta nu re*." That is how it should be.
"By the way, what is your name?" I asked.
"McKenzie." "Kankenze?" "No, McKenzie!"
We both got it without saying it; so relieved.
Thenceforth we had peaceful coexistence.

Dike Okoro
Remembering

1

The red soil of my childhood is engraved
on a stone in my mind. Muddy slides
driving children into playful shouts and dances
in the rain. I recall the thrill of anticipation.
Picking up a boneless earthworm with a stick
and gently tossing it over so it does not burst
open was an experiment that lasted for
as long as our eager hands and darting eyes
did not tire.

2

Following the rain, the cattle egrets took to the sky.
As we stared at them, we stretched out our small hands.
Chekeleke chekeleke, we sang, as we wished for
white patches on our fingers, as we warmed
to the departing flock in the dim light of
a bright day running away.

3

As night fell, we hiked home; home that loved
those it has forgotten. How do I say this without being
a leaf thirsting for sunlight, for it is only
when I welcome ambiguity that I experience
the solitude of bygone days! Joy leaping
out of memory's frying pan! Home, the udara
I eat in Chicago. Home, the fufu I buy
at the African store on Broadway Street, where
taxi drivers shopping for kola nut blast Rex Lawson's
highlife alongside Afrobeat mix tapes
on snowy December evenings.

4

In my imagination, their hearts compile messages
that are enchanting, like the messages they have
refused to let go because they entertain ghosts
from the past. I seek a reunion with those days,
seeing now how the burden of losing mother has
revived in me the need to treasure father. Fifty years
she tasted the salt of pains and ease with him and
danced to the drums of life in exile's endless carnival.

5

She who recounted stories to children and friends as the wind
whistled merrily. Her narratives served as testimonials
regarding an aunt deeply committed to mending the injured
and providing solace to the dying during the Nigerian Civil War.
Hands gripping leaves that have been crushed in a mortar.
Subsequently sprinkling them over exposed wounds on the torso,
as well as on the cavities created by bullets. When to live to see
another day meant to die a thousand deaths in fear, as bombs ripped
apart thatched houses. Bible clutched; lips moving. Amen! Until
dawn ambles in quietly, without cocks crowing; without birds
twittering. Dawn that carries the pleasant smile of the sun. Yes,
I see those days; the childhood I speak passionately about.

Victor Ola-Matthew
Another Man's Land

I. Chiropractor

Son of the land,
you are the first of them.
Your father, man of not-steel
and your mother, woman of not-steel
are breaking their backs for you.
You hear the cracking of their bones
in their weary voices over the phone
miles and miles away from you
and you are still reminded.
They need no chiro—you
You are enough to relieve these bones.
These bones that have known better days
like Oloibiri*,
like the wall of the ministries they have long served in
with pennies only enough for a magic trick.
The ache continues to ache regardless
as evil continues to perpetuate this government,
but you are hope in the land of the hopeless
Where they remain still—
tilling, back aching
singing, vocals failing.
dancing, blood pressure rising.

---

*Oloibiri is recorded as a small community in Nigeria's eastern Niger Delta region, Bayelsa
state, precisely, where crude oil was first discovered in 1956. However, Oloibiri, like many
communities housing oilfields in today's Nigeria, are in a state of severe environmental,
socio-economic, and cultural damage from decades of oil extraction and pollution. Oloibiri
has seen better environmental and socio-economic days, just like the bones and really
anything on Nigerian soil that has seen Nigeria dwindle, in that regard and many others, over
the years.

II. How to Be a Good Immigrant

You are African. Fullstop.
This is the first step to becoming
a good immigrant.
You are African,
Even if you are only certain of three North African countries.
You certainly can guess two more.
You are African,
Even if you have never tasted Ghanaian Jollof in Lagos.
You are African,
Even if you say, "my Ghana Must Go bag" casually
as if the phrase carries no magnitude, no history, no pain.
You are African,
Even if in your own country, tribes fail to get along.
Failure to understand yourselves—a governmental weapon.
You are African,
Even if tribal genocide is dancing behind you
like kids behind the reporter at a massacre scene
waiting for the microphone to be handed to them,
satisfied, knowing they will be seen.
You are African,
Even if you know little about your family tree
talk less of summarising a continent
all for TikTok content.
How else would they understand?
You are African—
Until you pull out that green passport
and realise you are different; by association, a 419 threat.

III. Demon of Might

No one will tell you
that in the scarcity of riches
there is a demon you must wrestle
before leaving for another man's land.
Denial denial denial.
This demon is only conquerable by acceptance.
Not denial.
Let him into you—accept that.
Accept that this might be the last time you
hug your mother, brother, and lover;
That they might die sooner than you can be reunited;

That for the not-rich like you,
the reunion might be a myth.
Accept that you might be too
busy securing your future, chasing a permanent residency
you might just miss their funeral.
The demon of might.

IV. Non-Player Characters

Non-player characters walking across the street
No footstep is heard as music is blared
Privately, into your pointy ears.
This new land is the street
And (it feels) you're the only real one on it.
The story of a new, lonely, hopeful immigrant.

Omotayo Olaoye
King Samba of Wazombia

I once knew of a king
That never stopped to sing
Of what the future will bring.
His voice sounded like thunder
And his songs stung like adders.
His hands were made of iron,
And his face, like that of a lion.
At his name the people trembled
And hearing his praise, they stumbled.
The king claimed to have the power
That would make him rule forever.
Every night he planned for tomorrow
And this put his people in sorrow.
But a night came when he slept
And so he slept till he was laid to rest.
His people praised the King of Kings.

Samba is an imaginary name given to a popular king in the poem. The name Samba is
symbolic, referencing the African drum, and alluding to the adage that a drum that sounds
too loud may burst. There is no king without a kingdom, so Wazobia in the title represents a
group of people under his rule.

Omotayo Olaoye
Strange Noises from the Embassy

The grains and tares are fully grown.
But we cannot reap. And we cannot weed.
For all our tools have broken down.
Their drugs have been prescribed,
But we lack consent to buy.
We settle for fish's raincoats instead
Because the nutrition from them is high.
We paint our floor white
In order to win the Elegance Award.
Our bodies are naked and wrinkled.
And our clothes hang above the fence.
Our name, fading and sinking.
But the nickname, reigning and shining,
Radiating the odours and colours
That made our fellows hate our contact.
They almost denied our coming to their land!

Frank Olunga
Dear Mother

I swam like my life depended on it.
Braved the crocodiles, cold ice water, no heat.
There were days when the heartbeat ceased.
I held on to hope of a foreign land
Free from the hell we were in.

Mother, your son made it to the other side,
The land they claimed was the land of milk and honey.

Mother, nights were like sword running through fresh wound.
Days were not as promising as we imagined.

Mother, I swam like my life depended on it.

Here, Mother, we smile even when we don't.
They whisper when they see me. They make way.
If you see me, you will wonder who I am.
I work for less, yet hours many, like stars in a clear night.
Here, I am not a human being. They call me an alien.
As we say at home, beggars can't be choosers.
So, I sleep in my single room where I must hide.
The sight of police makes my blood rush like a young river.
Operating at night like a witch, Mama,
I never stop thinking about you day and night.

Winter is like nothing I can explain. Bone freezing.

I don't want to bore you with my suffering. Mother,

Dear mother, with each passing day, home I miss.
I never knew the new hell that awaits
When I go shopping. They give me free security.
Someone to watch what I buy. My skin, the issue.

Mama, did you know you can buy guns like sweats here?
People are depressed and they need pills to sleep.
The land of milk and honey must have been a lie.
Everywhere, walks someone homeless. Imagine!

Mama, you and I know the truth of that day.

As they threw stowaways, you were swallowed by the ocean.
I saw as water made a feast out of you, Mama,.
You are watching from heaven above.

How's home?

I feel like a branch cut off from the source.
Every day, the fever kills me slowly, without warning.

Dear Mother, is there space for me by your side?
Somewhere where my worries will reside.

Mama, I won't let your spirit down. I won't.
I will live for both of us, mother. For both of us.

Alexander Opicho
Inside a Euro-Tunnel

        sea-gates and ports all blocked to your skin
        in your jostle
brethren
        to crash into Europe
the sole energy of your blind appetite
        look now you die like a rat and dragonfly
        inside the deathly heat of euro-tunnel
a living African is better than a dead migrant
        Europe is no guarantee that you will get rich
let's stay here and fight as a spirited team
                against all odds that betray African dreams
                power—corruption and male presidency   one life
                cradles of poverty   of technology and affluence
let's fight them with spirit of crossing euro-tunnel
and if we all die in the battle-field   no regret
        we take it like death inside the euro-tunnel

Omobola Osamor
Tomorrow on today's plate

Black chugs behind the *keke napep*,
        erupting volcanoes burn our throats, eyes and nostrils;
        joining ranks with emissions from industrial cigarettes,
a murder of crows,
countering libations,
writing our obituaries.

They sign referendum after referendum
        while poisons ink our veins,
        our bones become glass and skin parchment paper;

crematorium eating tomorrow on today's plate.

_____

Keke napep is a motorized three-wheeled vehicle powered by fuel.

Omobola Osamor
You Threw Yourself Away

Hope is a hatchling cracking through sand,
abandoning its nest. Hope is a pebble
skimming across a still pond. Hope is a minnow
gasping for food. Hope is a wolf
howling at the moon. Hope leaves a bed of broken shells
to quell a need it knows well.

Cast your shadow on the blue sea,
anchor thighs straddling the deep,
nets cast forth, mouth fuji dancing,
praying for fish—
claiming what the galaxy promises,
oysters in your eyes.
An eagle halts the hatchling's dream.
The pebble sinks into the deep.
The minnow swallows the hook.
A bullet halts the wolf's song.

Anchored thighs straddling the deep, you threw yourself away,
nets cast forth, praying for fish. You threw yourself away
hoping for what the galaxy promises. You threw yourself away,
oysters in your eyes.

This poem was birthed from the sense of horror I experienced after reading a news report
in January 2025 about three children who drowned in the Mediterranean Sea trying to
reach Europe. ('3 young African brothers drown in the Mediterranean Sea trying to reach
Europe, rescue group say', *CBS News*, 27 January 2025. Accessible at:
https://www.cbsnews.com/news/african-brothers-drown-mediterranean-crossing-rescue-
group/ [accessed: 3 November 2025]

Omobola Osamor
A Refugee's Prayer

Oba's exit from home didn't come with a manual.
The desert swallowed his footprints.
The imprint in his heart
he passed to Adeoti,
who followed the blueprint to Ìmọ́lẹ̀.

On, and on,
to the constellation of stars beneath the sky.

My ancestor sought life across the desert—
skin burnt raw beneath an unrelenting sun
— dispersed by Him who planted me
at the shore that unfurled my father.

Ìmọ́lẹ̀ literally translates to 'light' but can mean divine.

Ọba means king. Any name with the suffix 'Ade' translates to crown or something precious.

Adeoti means the crown does not fade.

Annette Pateman
First Time

The first time I felt
dark iron
on my wrists
around my neck
I thought
I was dying
Travelling to the
world of the dead
to be with
my ancestors
Instead it was
the living who had
enslaved my body
On plantations
of white cotton
where Black hands
pick pick pick
A place of
sweet sugar cane
turned to dark
molasses
Stickiness cloying
my heart
My mother tongue
sounds secret words
whispered in the dark
away from master's ear
The whip speaks
It shouts
submit submit submit!
Yet it does not
break me
Through drumbeats
food and my hairstyles
and the African rhythms of
a new created language
I find my way
back to
African blood memory

Elly Ray
The Search

A traveler I was born to be
A foreigner to every land

Since childhood, I looked tirelessly
For a place to call home
A place to lay my tired soul

I called many places home
But a foreigner, they called me instead
And I was faced with rejection every time

I called a distant land mine
The same way I rejected my land
The same way I said, I am better than this!

So, I kept looking and my agony grew bigger
And I found myself tired of embracing
What denies me the embrace
I found myself trapped in a land that needs me the most,
But I like it the least

So, I started looking for me within
The wreckage of a place I ought to accept
And I learned ultimate love the hard way

Elly Ray
Homeland Strays

In a land far away, where cultures collide,
There lived a girl, with her soul untied.
Her first language, foreign to her peers;
Her roots, a mystery, a puzzle indeed.
Raised in a different land, she felt out of place,
Yearning for a connection, a familiar space.
Deep in her heart, a longing unfolds.
Homesickness in her own home evolves.
Oh, she's alone, denying her call,
Rejecting her heritage, afraid to stand tall.
Lost in the shadows of doubt and despair,
dwelling in the past, burdens to bear.
In a third-world zone, trapped, she questions her fate.
"Why me?" she weeps, seeking an escape.
But within her tears, a strength defending against the malaise,
A fire within her, refusing to fade.
She fought through the darkness, each thought so bleak,
Resilient and determined, her spirit did speak.
She shrugged off criticisms, and the scorns that came,
For she knew her worth, and it fueled her flame.
Amidst the wreckage of hope, she sought to see,
The art and beauty that lie beyond the realm.
Oh, in the strayed, she discovered her calling's grace:
To show her land's beauty, alluring, and ablaze.
Baby steps she took, towards accepting her place,
Embracing her heritage, finally finding her peace.
She painted landscapes with words of pride,
Unveiling her culture, the colours so bright.
Her purpose now clear, she stood strong,
A beacon of inspiration, right where she belonged.
So, let's talk about this girl, her journey so profound,
From denial to acceptance, her growth unbound.
A storyteller, an ambassador of her own,
She showed the world the beauty she had known.
So, let her tale inspire. Let her spirit ignite.
In the depths of uncertainty, find your own light.
For within the strayed, there's a purpose to find,
And like the girl, let your purpose unwind.

Eric Rugara
Sibboleth

Then they would say to him, "Then say, 'Shibboleth'!" And he would say, "Sibboleth," for he could not pronounce it right. Then they would take him and kill him at the fords of the Jordan. There fell at that time forty-two thousand Ephraimites.

~Judges 12:6

swords find their targets
in fields of warm blood
dripping fear at dusk
where men lose resolution
and sons behold mothers humbled

the agony of lost hope
when hell is desirable
in a reality worse than nightmare
where screams drown in the
slash of machete through flesh

hordes descend upon us
neighbourly faces uglied
chanting hatred, murder
robots to men on podiums
messages in guise of violence

before the swords
was the leaflets
days of agonied suspense
nights of sleepless waiting
for the bloody inevitable

the men with the swords
us in the camps fleeing
both pawns in a game
pieces in an evil arithmetic
where elites play chess with lives

Mudadi Saidi
Refugee Woman

You ask who walks in shadows here?
She is a refugee woman, strong and clear.
From fifteen nations, she has fled
To Turkana West, where hope seems dead.

In semi-arid lands where sun beats down,
She searches for firewood, mile by mile.
Through rivers, she walks without a frown.
Facing danger, yet she keeps her smile.

Kidnapped, broken, bruised along the way.
Waiting for water that may never flow.
Living in anguish, day after day.
Her spirit bends but will not bow.

Her life's a battle in this camp of tears.
Queuing for medicine, for meager bread.
Sometimes beaten. Adding to her fears,
Four cereal packets keep her children fed.

She suffers deeply in the dust and heat.
Lives without promise of tomorrow's light.
When aid arrives, corruption makes it fleet.
Percentages stolen in the dead of night.

They call her "refugee woman" with disdain.
Dependable soul treated with such shame.
Many judge her story, few know her pain.
Few understand the fire within her flame.

But let me speak the truth that must be heard:
A refugee woman is like you and me.
A soul unbroken by each bitter word.
A woman rising, strong and proud and free.

She stands as cornerstone of this world's frame,
In this universe of sorrow that we share.
A woman who has never lost her claim
To dreams and visions. Mission beyond compare.

A woman who has honored life complete,
No matter what storms have crossed her path.
Her journey, born of war's bitter defeat.
Conflict and politics unleashed their wrath.

Where does she belong in this wide earth?
Right here, like any soul beneath the sun.
She deserves dignity, love, and worth.
Let us stand with her until justice is won.

Deborah Saki
Blood and Sugar of Home

I

From the plane's tiny window:

Its wing— defiant,
Like the people to whose country I travel.
The spirits of my people as dark shadows,
Across the blood red of sunrise.
And clouds like cotton candy,
Without the sugar of home.
From the plane's tiny window,
They, long gone, also watch me go.

II

Let me tell you about those nights when the moon is a plate in the sky,
And my longing blossoms, stretching out to fit my skin.
When home is a mere memory I trace in the stars,
A ghost of a place in the scent of magnolia.
Those nights when the rugged rust roads of home,
Running into my dreams promise to take me back—
Back to the place that publishes the rituals of care,
And the citations of love.
Those nights when home beckons to me,
Through the winking stars and the wailing wind
On those nights, when the moon is a plate in the sky,
What is there to keep from falling apart?

III

I wrap my intentions in the brightly colored fabrics of my home,
(And) fold them into the recesses of my heart,
when the officer at the immigration desk asks, "What
Is your business here?"
I say my letters well-rehearsed—
The degree, the research, the advancement of science.
Against his probing gaze
I bid my intentions: lie still.
Not to stir, restless within themselves,
Lest they reveal themselves as the dark shadows in my pupils,
As the red in my eye
Or slip out of my mouth,
And stain my lips with the color of ambition, of lies,
Of a new name, a new country, a new passport.

Deborah Saki
A New City

I read about a thing—
a phenomenon

They said sometimes when you have a baby
the abdominal walls
can separate

I wonder,

Does it happen to hearts?

When you have longing
when there is distance between love
the walls of my heart are stretched out

Everywhere I turn there are new faces
Mum, dad

No hugs

I am wandering in a new city

I talk about the way a new country strips you naked

Where your home was a blanket
that you wore well

Your new land is a fashionable dress,
it's showing your legs and curves

You're beautiful

But you're cold

Why did we leave?

We left for far off visions in the corners of our consciousness
Blurry images that made our hearts jump but which we could not identify
Emotions we tasted on our tongues but could not name
They tasted like promises and ambitions and freedom, but not exactly
Words that murmured in our veins that we could not place our fingers on

We did not leave for the flat white pills in their transparent orange tubes
that the doctors say may make you drowsy, may reduce your sex drive,
may give you sleep problems, weight changes
follow up with me in three weeks
Or the nights we would stay awake stretching into the ceiling,
becoming one with the night
Wake with bags the size and weight of loneliness
Hours spent in front of the woman with the curly hair, *LPC*
Telling us to breathe deeply, practice gratitude
Not for empty laughter, quiet rides home and the sound of silence

But sometimes the weather is nice, and the flowers bloom differently here
Purple and pink and blue
Like they never did back home

Partha Sarkar
Long Live Livelihood

Alone, meets the panel
To check the names.

Who should be guillotined by the project?

A long queue.
The dilapidated faces.

The countless documents
Submitted by non-entities.

Comes the long drawn carriage
To take the documented to the tomb
As, after a while, there will be a vacant place
As most of the headless pregnant
Will be thrown out
And none cares to cry.

Partha Sarkar
Innocents Are Either Dead or Escapists

Prevails on the entire death
the ceasefire.

A grey way of living.

Three stairs of the whore-monger
And all go upstairs
And none can come downstairs.

The living boiled potato.

Flies half of phosphorus to the other life.

Remains of the ages
the span of life under the freezing point.

The cold grains in the yard
no pigeons touch them.

Welcomes death,
the ceasefire.

James Sentiba
A Promise of Hope

The greatest joy is dreaming with your eyes wide open.
It's hoping with a vengeance so sharp, you slice through mountains
Destroying conventions and preconceived notions
And creating solutions to abate the tribulations.
All we can do is create and make into existence
Portfolios of renewal and reckoning, of renaissance and resistance.
A new age is coming when time will fold and break upon herself
And all that we've lost here will coalesce to a river belt
Of lush green abundance.
And light will emanate from the soil
Bursting forth in kaleidoscopic wonder,

James Sentiba
Swamp Song

nothing left to say, nothing left to do
when all hope is lost and there's nothing
left to lose
I'll therapize myself like I always do
and make jokes about the future
paths I'm bound to choose.

***

Relegate me to the forgotten chorus
of crickets that sing in the swampy marsh.
I am home among the creeping vines.
Like curls tangled between silver prongs,
I make the palms my resting place.
Nothing can harm me here
in the weeping wetland where
music and wind are the only languages.
I float on the wind, humming in unison
with the swaying palm leaves.

Ndaba Sibanda
as long as

she had the liberty
to live where she thought
the sun, her sun
radiated rays of fun

– where she would not
tomorrow sorrow
for having wandered
off into an infinite dimness
or into a house whose roof was full
of holes and hurt
instead of happiness –

she had the right to migrate
like a seasonal bird in winter,
to soar and sing her best songs,
to like the firmament she wanted,
to live the abundant life she desired,
– for we live once, we merit the best –

she had the autonomy to serenade
a deeper tune with a life of its own,
to sing a melody of love she favored,
to form and frequent the best nest
she was enamored and comfy with –

she had the freedom to be a bird,
to fly cheek high in the sky,
to sing the sundrenched song she desired
and dance with a voice full of vitality,
to sing as long as that voice was hers
– for cynical voices have no cadence –

yes, as long as her wise wings
did not act up and spin off
and see her happy heart
hurtle down a highway
of hurt or heartache –

as long as she took responsibility
– for liability is the heir of maturity –
yes, as long as that life was hers,
for it has to be lived and loved

Ndaba Sibanda
s(t)(c)reams of splendor

away from the hurry
and the hum and the strain
and the pain of his home city,
he was in a hamlet, playing catchup
with mental calmness and cleanliness,
yes, with the bloom and beauty of nature,
the brooks, the roaring river and its tireless,
tiny, twisty tributaries   he gazed with reverential
admiration interspersed with trepidation, curiosity
and wonder at the graceful, gushing, laughing river
and heard its seamless series of euphoria and its streamflow
he noticed the flow was resisted by the butted rocks and the soil
that made up the river bed and how the flow determined the shape
and behavior of the river system, leaving him exclaiming, awestruck,

Palmwine Sounds
Kunta Kinte

Kunta Kinte
He hailed
From The
Gambia

The African
A fierce warrior
Strong, proud
Well-educated

Kunta Kinte
Was sailed
To faraway
To Slave

The African
Was flogged
Overworked
And not paid

Kunta Kinte
Was forced
Bearing seeds
For the enslaver

The African
Forgotten
His home
Colonised

Kunta Kinte
Wise up now
Marginalised
For too long

Palmwine Sounds
The Green, Red, Black and Gold

Wave your flag with Pride
The African Nation

Green
The land is too fertile and rich
The wealth is immeasurable

Red
The blood of our prophets
The blood of the oppressed

Black
Our colour so bold
United down to our DNA

Gold
The diversity of culture and religion
Peace and harmony we dream of

Cindy Steward
immigration generation

I

our passports have different colours,
and they said i was lucky to see
the purple tones that contrast
their greens so vividly,

and i am embarrassed when they ask
me where i am from, and i express a
country i have been to twice, and have
no legal connections to,

and i am proud when i distance myself
from the country my parents worked so hard
to integrate into, because i have never felt
at home, i have never felt i was a citizen

so i request a visa for the third time, and
visit the home i have been told to have and miss
as much as it hasn't missed me

II

their goodbyes were exchanged, in the form
of a see-you soon that never arrived,
so my second-generational identity
could be honed by creating independency
that they have never understood,
as it is so culturally significant
and abandoned,
and we wonder

"i want to live"
"i want to leave"
"i envy"
"i miss"
"i owe"
"i give"
"i took"

and we are thankful that
their existence gave ours
a meaning that differs
so greatly from those before

and we wonder
what to do with it

Cindy Steward
it matters

when it flows to
the circumstances of
our meanings
our societal repetitions
and creative dedications
familial separations
or loving citations
we remember when
it matters

i miss those days
and look forward to
those ahead
to shape an identity
worth inhabiting
to create an essence
worth filling
continuously

i'll ask you, next time,
what you think of
those words
and recite them
to make sure you
know their
meanings

then
we'll decide
together

SuAndi
Intergenerational Trauma

My father first walked the earth in Warri
His feet sinking into the hot mud of Nigeria's Delta State
Then one day, as other men launched fishing boats
He sailed far away.
Why, I don't know,
He never told me,
I never asked.
Africa and Manchester did not offer life parallels
So we never had that conversation

My father never talked of the past
I never asked
What did you do in the war dad?
What was your home like?
Do I look like your people?
Can you see your mother in my eyes?
The way I walk, argue
I'm a female version of you
Am I the same height as your father?
Words never spoken
Only got silent responses.

My father never said
When the white man came:
But I know he knew.
Summers we would visit his old master
Exchanging our terrace house
For a large white detached in Richmond Surrey
Where my father cleaned;
A servitude repayment for our visit.
While I was forbidden to
Touch, speak, play,
Do anything without first asking permission.
Strange white people I thought.
"Snobby bastards," said my mother when I returned home
"Where do they think this is?
It's not bloody Africa."
Her temper causing her cheeks to flame red
Matching the copper of her hair
"Andi," she'd say

"Slavery is over;
Get over it."
What did she mean?
But I never asked
And she never explained.

Schools for my father
Were glorious European opportunities
So he spared nothing to buy
My uniform, my shoes
A too large briefcase.
Copies of the same books that teachers
Distributed daily in class.
Strange, that I had to leave the classroom
To begin my education;
Tutored via overheard conversations
Documentaries, radical articles
And orators from Marcus Garvey to Malcolm X.
Even though neither had a liking for white people.
But no matter how I broadened my knowledge,
I still loved my mother
Nothing was going to change that.
Now my mouth was full
Of words my brain had memorised
Colonialism, lynchings, detention
Apartheid, segregation
Civil Rights, Black Power
And always
Slavery.

What did my father know?
That the Yoruba's were favoured for their strength
But whipped long to curb their independence
That the Ibos though stolen in their thousands
Also found an inner power to walk on water
And the Ijaw from Warri
Who speaks of them?
Not, certainly my father.
Except sometimes,
When the silence was so loud my ears would ache
I would turn to him
And he looking far into the distance
Seemed oblivious to the tears

Washing his cheeks
Flowing under his chin
Then water falling towards his heart.

In that moment my father
Was no longer the man I knew
The man I didn't know.
He was in that moment,
A body filled with the spirits of all his ancestors.
My family from my grandfather
To generations who never imagined life beyond the Forçados River
Conquered, shackled, bartered
Sold, abused, demonised, throttled, burnt, flogged
Criminalised, imprisoned,
Executed by the law under the law.

The trauma of the new
The wicked the evil
Filled my father
So that he could not speak
And I never asked why.
Why,
Before he died
Was he called Thomas

Under my right eye
I have an indentation
It is in the exact same place
As my father's peoples' ritual scarring
Some days when I look at it
It seems more prominent
Like it really is a scar
But I can barely make it out
Through my tears

Sheila Thadani
Rights Abridged

We seek our dreams across the ocean.
Like a flock of birds, we leave our nests,
Drawn by the light of a shining beacon.

The rights and ideals we hold dear
Sound like gentle voices in the ear.
To our rights abridged, we sing this song.
From the ancestral land, we belong.

Graced by nature's carpet of colour,
Our lands were not born for verve
But as a place for ease and languor.

We learnt to train body and mind,
To feel empathy for all and be kind.
Compassion and truth was our quest,
But without reason we were oppressed.

We aimed to replace distress with calm,
But were subjected to danger and harm.
What benefit had anyone to gain
From dictates of unjust constraint?

Hope rises like the morning sunrise,
With its welcoming arms of joy,
As we leave with no regrets or sighs.

We should care and we should grieve
When they punish us for benign beliefs.
We should fight for rights to maintain,
Not imprison, cull organs or inflict pain.

We sail to shores with a vision,
Braving storms and surging seas,
Yet wait to fulfill our mission.

You ask why should we care?
We all have a duty, to be fair,
To use our sphere for oversight,
When humans are denied basic rights.

Dreams take time to reach their goal.
They meander around rocks and hills
Before they assume their precious role.

Endowed we are with so short a life,
Do we squander it all on strife?
Or allow wisdom into our hearts and minds,
To live in peace with what is left of time?

Like vines that forever twine
To reach their glory, a new land
Bears its harvest only after a time.

Sheila Thadani
Slaughter of An African King

Cecil was a famous black-maned lion in Zimbabwe's Hwange National Park. In 2015, he was lured out of the park by an American recreational big-game trophy hunter who wounded him using a compound bow. The trophy hunter then tracked and killed Cecil the following morning, 10 to 12 hours later.

Blue surfs entice to lands
Of mystery. Forests and groves,
Where nimble chimps clamber
Trees, and animals burrow.

Elephants reach out to befriend.
Sweltering monsoon saturates the terrain.
Deep in the jungle, lush feather ferns
Stretch out to touch.

There, eyes unseen, watch from
Cracks and crannies. In the thick
Of forest leaves, and the rustle of
A whispering breeze, lay Cecil, the lion.

A majestic head with flowing
Fur rising from his body of amber;
The dark mane's straggly hair
Hidden under a bushy lair.

Enthroned with nature's coronet,
A roar that crowned him King,
With awe from all those living,
Feared by all as a threat.

Bushy thickets of dense woods
Since birth, was his home;
Plains where he always roamed
At the water's edge for food.

On this fateful day,
As Cecil gazed into space,
Predators hid a distance away
With deadly weapons in place.

One shot fired from the crossbow

condemns the lion to a long night of agony
Before the trophy hunter returns and ends his reign.
An African King hauled away as someone's trophy.
A looted life.

Patrick Kapuya Tshiuma
Until Again Goma is Free!

Goma was not Gomorrah,
Yet it burned to ashes.
Bullets rained as mothers wept.
Rebels were thirsty for loot.

We survived the wrath of Nyiragongo,
The sky aglow, smoke in our lungs.
Tears carved paths we couldn't hide.
On Congo's land, wounds are carved too wide.

Whether you were twenty or three,
Only death could set you free
That day, January twenty-eight.
Who could we blame, but M23?

Once, we believed that life was fair.
We drew our hopes in lines of care.
Now truth is far, trapped in despair and lies
With no hope, too tired even to cry.

Goma was no Sodom.
Few sins. It was no Gomorrah.
Lakes and peaks where peace had been,
Bombs dropped while flowers blossomed.

We screamed and begged for mercy.
A paradise shelled from the skies.
Heaven turned its face away
As we counted our dead that day.

Desecrated, pillaged, shamed.
Some fled, others crucified.
Our tender home, by war, defamed.
Many stayed. And many fell, petrified.

Why? we asked, but silence roared.
Ghosts roamed with hearts depleted.
We sought their eyes. Void. They ignored. Black.
Their souls, they sold, for peace to never come back.

Goma became our Pandora.
A box flung open by horror.
Coltan and gold unleashed a storm.
But the mines were mine from before I was born.

Foxes came with fangs and fire.
The fields became a funeral pyre.
Axes and fury rose. A morbid stench.
From trenches, a putrid scent.

Goma was never meant as hell.
It was a place where angels dwelled.
Its beauty, pure. Its silence, deep.
Too sacred for wolves to keep.

Goma was heaven. Once serene.
Corpses drifting across the lake
As Goma fell in the fog. A dantesque scene.
I lived. Now in my coma, I cannot wake,

For God's sake,
Until again Goma is free!

This poem is inspired by a horrific event that occurred on January 28, 2025, in the Democratic Republic of Congo, my home country: the capture of the city of Goma by the Rwandan-backed M23 terrorist group. This attack on the city was accompanied by massive human rights violations and killings that claimed the lives of 8,000 people in just four days. Although still in shock, I wanted to talk about it. Perhaps these few words will help ease my pain.

Patrick Kapuya Tshiuma
The Long Way Home

Here comes a new spring
See the flying sparrows

We've crossed deserts and seas
The forests
Left behind our shadows

Let us forget the sorrow
And think about tomorrow

In God we trust
His mercy we seek
His path and word we follow

His breath we borrow
Time and space, he owns all

When the sky turns black
To the earth he shows his love

Into the valley of darkness
Down the stream of hope, let us all flow

Our homes and families we shall bless
And our enemies not to curse

He cleared the way and set me free
My pride I have to swallow

From the dust he raised me
And He made me a hero

From evil his child he spared
I survived for I am his spear

In the moment of war and despair
In my heart he planted no fear

He kept me from warlords
From right-wing hatred, hardcore
From Jungle beasts and narcos

I did not die a John Doe

Under his wings I am safe
By his grace I live and wish

Upon his name I call with rage
Through his spirit I found forever peace

He is the sun one shall never gaze at,
For thy face by his ray shall set ablaze

Maweeja Nnangila

Maweeja Nnangila is the name of God in Ciluba, my mother tongue, which is spoken in the Kasai region of the Democratic Republic of Congo. In the Luba tradition, it is customary to conclude a poem by invoking God.

Philisiwe Twijnstra
Zulu Girl In Rotterdam

i.
TIME negotiation BEGINS.
Thirty weeks. Seven months.
Two hundred and eleven days.
Five thousand, one hundred ten hours.
In the sea of whiteness, the body floats. Drifts in foreign land.
The city whispers she's black.

—*Sorry, Ik spreek Nederlands niet, Yes English Please*

ii.
The body tumbles down.
The black forgotten body is bruised.
The body aches for air.
Narrow stairs.
She sits in the bedroom.
Wait...
Shortage of houses, Show gratitude.
She sits in *her* bedroom.
Cold seeps through her bones.
Sitting in the room with a bed.
Thirty showers of rain.
Four white flurries of snow.
Two battering hails.
Three ferocious winds.
Five hopeful rays of sunshine.
She's the loneliest Zulu girl in Rotterdam.
Frozen in bed. Longing to hear —

Sawubona.

Sawubona is a Zulu greeting that translates to "I see you". The greeting implies a deeper connection, suggesting that by being seen, the individual truly exists..

iii.
to those who believed they knew the sun.
like a drug dealer, you take pills.
oh, mothers in a black church.
chorus girls, with white sneakers, red beret & bibles.
flaky skin on a pillow.
Vaseline Blue Seal, where are you Vaseline Blue Seal?
you thought you knew the sun.
the sun you thought you knew, didn't know you.
the sun is not the same.
it snows after the sun.
this sun does not have clan names.
this sun has no beginning.
this sun has no morning.
it is not the same.

Ijeoma Victory Ejme
The Prisoner

In a foreign land, I wander
far beyond the borders
in pursuit of the green
that my eyes haven't seen

Do I have to beg
for my life fragile like an egg
my feet chained to the floor
while I stare at the wall without a door

Do I have to cry
while my blood runs dry
I writhe on the ground
my hands tightly bound

Do I have to dream
past a reality so grim
in a land I came to see
far beyond the sea

Do I have to hope
to be free of these ropes
that have tied me since the day
I stepped my feet at Bay

Do I have to shout
screams from my mouth sprout
my lips made of clay
utter words my heart pray

in a foreign land I wander
far beyond the borders
in pursuit of the green
that my eyes haven't seen

Ijeoma Victory Ejme
So Much For So Little

He was sitting silently, his eyes so bright
against the black of his skin, at the edge,
a little away from me, in the crowd
of fellows with whom we grasped for air
in the waters of the Mediterranean.
It was his calm quietness, in the midst
of the harrowing screams,
that drew me to him.
I called to him.
He laughed.
He pointed to a body floating in the sea.
"So much for so little," he said.
"He is the son of my mother.
"My brother. I lost him to a land
"where I will become nothing."

Faresi Yasini
If only...

If only I had it my way,
I would change everything.
I would change everything that brings pain and sorrow.

If only I had it my way,
I would give everything.
I would give everything that everyone needs and desires.

If only I had it my way,
I would take everything away.
I would take everything away that gives power to the wrong people.

If only I had it my way,
I would make this real.

Faresi Yasini
African Woman Dreams of Freedom

I am woman,
sister, mother, world citizen,
human.

Everywhere
I am ignored,
judged,
neglected,
abused,
the colour of my skin and gender,
the excuse and justification.

I am woman,
sister, mother, world citizen,
human.

My voice is as strong
as the colour and texture of my skin.
I was here in the beginning.
My voice can be heard across time and space.

I will not change my skin.
I will not lower my voice.
I will use my voice until I am heard.

I am woman,
sister, mother, world citizen,
human.

Gorrety Yogo
Mimi Fly's Rich

After high school in Kabondo, Mimi decided to look for work in Eldoret where her aunt stayed. This way she could save for upkeep.

While in Eldoret, she could not find a job.

She had to move to Nairobi upon finding a job as a househelp through a friend.

In Nairobi, she heard about employment agents who assist in the migration processes to Qatar for better salaries. She was so overjoyed.

She told her parents who were happy.

She applied and now works in Qatar where she sends money home but complains of overworking.

Furaha Youngblood
You Need To Let It Go!

Unbearable burdens of racism, poverty, and injustice
Trigger thoughts of violent rebellion, that expressed,
Frighten the ungodly to offer their version of
Christian forgiveness as a way to keep the peace:
"You need to let it go."

To us,
It is simply *deja vu*.

Our language,
We had to let it go.

Our family,
We had to let it go.

Our freedom,
We had to let it go.

Our land,
We had to let it go.

Our very self,
We had to let it go.

Our gods,
We had to let them go.

Forgiveness is overrated.

Our insistence that "Black Lives Matter,"
We will not let it go!

Our demands for justice,
We will not let it go!

Our determination to end police brutality,
We will not let it go!

Our actions to nullify white supremacy,
We will not let it go!

Our efforts to build strong, healthy communities,
We will not let it go!

Our fight to reclaim our humanity,
We will not let it go!

Furaha Youngblood
Adrift

Adrift. Clueless. Unconscious.
I am lost in a landscape without familiar landmarks:
Sahara Desert sand; Mt. Kilimanjaro snow;
Atlantic Ocean waves; Ituri Forest trees.

My spirit drifts in foreign lands where the wilfully blind
refuse to see and accept my humanity.

Snip! Snip! Snip!
Wigs. Bleaching creams. Blue contact lens.
Wool. Polyester. Spandex.

I have been locked into a dressing room filled with clothes that do not fit.
The dressing table holds round powder boxes filled
with shades that complement only cream and ivory skin tones.
Ebony, Chocolate, Cinnamon, and Caramel are foreign.
The FunHouse mirror is the only one I'm allowed to use;
the distorted images it gives back, are the only ones you will accept as real.
I am the ugly stepsister whose foot won't slip into the glass slipper.

Verdi. Mozart. Copeland

My drum, thumb piano, kora, banjo, balafon,
once rejected as profane, are now acceptable,
having been successfully transformed into
tympani, concert grand, guitar, xylophone.

Shakespeare. Dante. Dickinson.
King's English. Flawless French. Unaccented Spanish.

Stripped of my languages, denied platforms to tell my stories, my religions
(myths to you) found no outlet in your written words; thus, confining me
to the parochial, and less-respected spoken idioms.

Concrete. Steel. Plastic.
McDonald's, Taco Bell, Dunkin' Donuts
TSA. NSA. USA.
CNN. MTV. FOX.

These are your cultural and political markers; not mine.

There are no maps to help me find my way back to myself.
I am adrift in a sea of unfamiliar and frightful things.
Adrift.

Yet, to save myself, I must use the floating planks
of cultural imperialism, a sinking ship's debris.
I am powerless to choose otherwise.

Will my children's children understand?
Will they forgive? I do not want them to forget.

I am a survivor, and once ashore,
I will burn those planks to warm my spirit.

Kathy Zwick
Who Will Dare to Think Outside the Box?

Just born, happy arrival, welcome!
Your delighted *Bibi* and *Babu* welcome darling,
determined, daringly determined, little Ella Nuru
boldly greeting Dar es Salaam on a glorious, hot,
daringly hot, sun-blessed July day.

Talented graduate student, ardent anti-colonialist, eager,
curious, studious, daringly hopeful, young Julius Nyerere
arrives in cerebral misty Edinburgh, enthusiastic, speculating,
contemplating.

He searches for new ideas, meets Fabian texts,
imports them, adapting them to his young struggling country
of your birth. He blends and mixes, boldly experimenting,
juggling all those new and various ideas.

He melds Scottish Fabian optimism with tried and trusted years
of traditional Tanganyikan familyhood. He flirts with classical liberalism.
Ardently, he adapts from Thoreau and Mahatma Gandhi.
Those feisty foreign ideas migrate south to graft
with home grown African thinking, but when....

*In 1998 Julius Nyerere met with World Bank officials in Washington.
They asked him, "Why have you failed?"*

*He replied, "The British Empire left us a country with 85% illiterates, two
engineers and 12 doctors. When I left office, we had 9% illiterates and
thousands of engineers and doctors. I left office 13 years ago. Then our
income per capita was twice what it is today; now we have 1/3 less
children in our schools, and public health and social services are in ruins.
During these 13 years, Tanzania has done everything the World Bank and
IMF have demanded."*

*Nyerere then returned the question back to the World Bank experts, "Why
have you failed?"*

Dearest Ella Nuru,

In wearing your Swahili name, may there be
a joyous casting of light and a long and lasting opening of the mind.

In our mercurial world of changes and upheavals,
of coups and countercoups,
of floods and droughts, of toppled statues and graffitied gravestones,
of inequalities, of uneven surpluses, and unjust austerities,
who will dare to mine and mix philosophies,
who will dare to speak,
to think outside the box, who will dare to adapt and grow ideas,
to raise a voice – and to ask hard questions?

*Julius Nyerere (1922 – 1999), "Baba wa Taifu" (Father of the Nation),
First President of Tanzania (1962 – 1985)*

This poem, originally written to welcome my granddaughter, seemed to migrate into a
tribute to Julius Nyerere. He arrived in Edinburgh to expand his learning. A popular, much-
admired student, he acquainted his fellow students and teachers with African ideas. He
returned home with a new and blended kit of political and economic theories and adapted
many to his dreams of building a unified, peaceful, and proud Tanzania.

CONTRIBUTORS

Oluwaseyi Adebola (MBBS, MSc. MRCS) is a Nigerian trained doctor currently working as a neurosurgery specialty registrar in Liverpool. He has a master's degree in translational neuropathology from Sheffield & a distinction in advanced diploma in creative writing from Tennessee. Oluwaseyi is the author of a collection of short stories titled *A Cluster of Petals* which was shortlisted for the 2019 Quramo Writer's award and the 2019 Afire Linda Ikeji Prize for literature. He is also the founder and curator of CreativeNaija.com, a social network/marketplace for creative Nigerians via which he curated the work, *I Am Nigeria: An anthology of what it means to be Nigerian in past, present and future tenses*. He is a contributing author for *African Ghost Short Stories* and his works have appeared in international and local platforms including Papercuts and Itanile.

Abiola Agbaje is a passionate writer, dedicated professional and an individual who likes to advocate for empathy and social consciousness. She's currently on the path of honing her storytelling skills and enjoys lots of quiet time as well as playing car race games.

Jim Aitken is a poet and dramatist living and working in Edinburgh. He is a tutor in Scottish Cultural Studies with Adult Education and he organises literary walks around the city. His last poetry collection was *Declarations of Love*, published in 2022. Jim is a widely published poet and Associate Editor with Culture Matters.

Rina Malagayo Alluri has been rooted, uprooted and replanted in various soils. She is a Filipina-South Indian poet, peace scholar and yoga practitioner who grew up between Ibadan, Nigeria and Vancouver, BC Canada/Turtle Island. She is currently Assistant Professor and UNESCO Chair in Peace Studies, University of Innsbruck, Austria. Her poetry weaves together experiences of (de)coloniality, diasporic identities and relationships that form/unform. Some recent work can be found in: *Beyond Words Magazine, Carnation Zine, Frontier Poetry, The Hemlock, Middleground Magazine and Yellow Arrow Publishing.*

Driss Amjich. Translator and Writer. Born in Morocco.

Gordon Anjili is a retired high school teacher who has taught English and Literature in six schools in five different counties of Kenya. He has written four unpublished plays.

Yemi Atanda is the author of *Dialectics of Revolution in the Postcolonial Drama of Obafemi & Yerima: Towards the Theory of Revalorization* (Scholar, 2014). He is a co-editor (Femi Osofisan & Abiola Fasoranti) of *The Time is Out of Joint: Playwriting in a Time of Global Incoherence* (Mosuro Publishers, 2016).

Amisah Bakuri (PhD) is a research associate at the Faculty of Religion and Theology, Vrije Universiteit Amsterdam. With more than 12 years of research experience, she specialises in various fields such as religion, migration, well-being, sexuality, gender, and the health of minority groups, particularly the Black and African diaspora.

Antje Bothin loves writing poetry. Her poems have been published in several international anthologies, journals and magazines. She authored an inspirational novel called *Annika and the Treasure of Iceland*. When not being creative, she can be found doing voluntary work in nature or drinking tea.

Yasmin S Brown is an international bestselling co-author, poet, and certified life coach. She received her coaching certificate from the International Coaching Federation. Yasmin utilizes her personal and healthcare professional experience to advocate for women's mental health. Through innovation, she brings organizational health, communication, and trauma-informed awareness worldwide.

M. Chambers, born in 1956, his working life was spent as a professional archaeologist, but is now retired. His short stories have won some prizes with the Federation of Writers (Scotland) and Luna Press, and have been long and short listed. His poetry has appeared in Lucent Dreaming, Poetry Space and some anthologies, including the Kistrech Festival. He now lives in Guisborough, England, on the edge of the North York Moors.

Barrington Gordon's poems and short stories address conundrums behind humanity's masks. His short story, "Grandfather's Feet" was published in *Whispers in the Walls: New Black and Asian Voices from Birmingham* (Tindal Street Press 2001), an anthology endorsed by Benjamin Zephaniah and Bonnie Greer. The story was also read and broadcast on BBC Radio 4. His work has been featured in anthologies and publications that include *Voice Memory Ashes: Lest we Forget* (Mango Publishing 1999), Steel Jackdaw: Edition 4 (2021), *Poetry and Settles Status for All* (CivicLeicester 2022), *Welcome to Britain: An Anthology of Poems and Short Fiction* (CivicLeicester, 2023), and in the Walsall Society of Artists' 73rd annual exhibition at the New Walsall Art Gallery (2024), and Art Meets Poetry, which curated his Ekphrastic poems twinned with artists' compositions as part of Wolverhampton's Annual Literature Festival.

Zainab M. Hassan is a poet, writer and human rights and gender equity activist. Zainab is the first ethnic Somali, and female poet featured in The Library of Congress' African Poet and Writers Event. Some of her poems were published on the Horn of Africa Journal (HoA), and Bildhaan Journal.

Zita Holbourne FRSA is a multi-award winning, multidisciplinary artist, author, educator, community activist, equality and human rights campaigner and trade union leader. Her creative practice includes work as a visual artist, performance poet, writer and vocalist. She has exhibited art, performed poetry and spoken around the globe.

Ugwuja Emmanuel Ifeanyichukwu, poet and short story writer, explores memory, music, and meaning. A UNN graduate, he won Eze's Paschal Short Story Prize (2024) and PIN's 10 Days of August Challenge (2024). His works, featured in The Muse and The Truth Magazine, reflect literature as emotion's truest mirror.

Zan V. Johns. Internationally Recognized Author of 3 poetry collections, 4 collaborative books, *What Matters Journal*, and featured in numerous anthologies and international literary publications. Website: www.zanexpressions.com

Nandi Jola was born in Gqebera, South Africa. She holds a Master of Arts degree in English (Poetry) from Queen's University, Belfast, Northern Ireland. Nandi is a poet, storyteller, playwright and creative writing facilitator, and is well known in Northern Ireland and beyond for her work in the Arts and Museum and Heritage sector. Nandi edited Issue 14 of Poetry Ireland's annual literary pamphlet, *The Trumpet*, and was curator of the Golden Shovel Poetry Jukebox. She is also a creative writing facilitator for Quotidian. Among her plays, the topically titled *Partition*, and *The Rise of Maqoma*, engage with and also seek to move beyond Eurocentric themes. https://www.doirepress.com/writers/nandi-jola

Samuel Julius Habakkuk Kargbo is a Sierra Leonean. He is popularly known as Rabbi, the Watchman, or God Poet. He was born in Wilberforce village, Freetown. He has a BSc in Chemistry from Fourah Bay College, US an MSc in Environmental Sciences (Hons) from Cyprus International University. He is currently researching Environmental Toxicology at Nagasaki University in Japan. He celebrates others as he loves to see people grow and metamorphose into butterflies.

Anton Krueger has published plays, memoir, short stories, criticism and arts journalism. Lately, he's been experimenting with spoken word collaborations with improvising musicians, including Tony Bental, Warrick Sony, Francois le Roux and Paul Hanmer. He lives in Makhanda where he heads the Department of Literary Studies in English at Rhodes University. To sample his work, visit: https://amateurist.weebly.com/writings.html

Thulani Mahlangu is from Pretoria in South Africa, and is a wanderer looking to change the world with his words.

Esther Mamadou, a migration and refugee lawyer, has been working on migration in the Mediterranean since 2004. Anti-Black racism activist, she advocates for the protection of the human rights and dignity of Africans migrating who suffer from deadly policies in a world where structural racism oppresses Black and racialized bodies.

Monica Manolachi lives in Bucharest, Romania, where she teaches English and Spanish at the University of Bucharest. She is a literary translator and a poet. She has published numerous articles on contemporary poetry and prose, and is the author of *Performative Identities in Contemporary Caribbean British Poetry* (2017).

Leonora Masini is a scholar of Fascist History and European Colonialism. She works primarily on documentary films representing life under colonial rules. She is interested in collective memories of colonial times, how we preserve them, and how we cope with their presence.

Octavia McBride-Ahebee's poetry is informed by the convergence of cultures and the many ways people move throughout the world. She presents relationships within the context of global inequality.

Karuna Mistry is a British writer from Leicester who's been published in 70+ anthologies with >100 individual poems. He has two poetry books, "You-me-*verse*-all *Hue*man" (2025) and debut, "Sojourn: Transcending Seasons" (2024) https://www.instagram.com/karunamistrypoetry/

Jenny Mitchell won the Gregory O'Donoghue Prize 2023, and the Poetry Book Awards for *Map of a Plantation*, a Manchester Metropolitan University set text. The prize-winning collection, *Her Lost Language,* is One of 44 Poetry Books for 2019 (Poetry Wales). Her latest collection, *Resurrection of a Black Man*, contains three prize-winning poems.

Nasra Dahir Mohamed holds an MPhil in Public Policy from Ripham International University, Islamabad, Pakistan, along with a dual Bachelor in Political Science and International Relations from the Civil Service Institute, Somaliland, and a BSc in Medical Laboratory from Edna Adan University, Somaliland. Over the years, Nasra has accumulated experience in research coordination, translation, and transcription for various international, local, and governmental organizations, as well as Ph.D. students.

Mariam Mohammed is a Ghanaian, who is currently a graduate student at the University of Tennessee. She loves to write short stories and poems on race, mental health, love, and grief.

Fauziyatu 'Fauzi' Moro is a 2024 Mellon/ACLS Fellow and PhD candidate at the University of Wisconsin-Madison. She is an urban and social historian specializing in 19th and 20th-century West Africa, with research interests in African urban migration and women and gender history.

Remind Mugwambani was born in 2001, in Kwekwe, Zimbabwe. He is the third of four children. His published works include "Today is Your Day, Go and Win," "Resilient Driver," and "I Will Be Home to Tell the Story," all of which were featured in the anthology *Wind on My Face: Motorcycle Diaries*.

Ambrose Musiyiwa is a poet and journalist with a background in the intersection between activism, migration, and community action. He coordinates Journeys in Translation, an international, volunteer-driven initiative that is translating *Over Land, Over Sea: Poems for those seeking refuge* (Five Leaves Publications, 2015) into other languages. Ambrose is also on the editorial board of the Africa Migration Report Poetry Anthology Series.

Francis Muzofa (aka @Pope) is a Zimbabwean poet. His poems have been published by various platforms both locally and internationally. He is a philosophical poet who uses humor, allegory and satire to poke into the eyes of witches. His writings are inspired by nature and the social ills that hurt the innocent and vulnerable. If he was God for a day, he would kill poverty and spread kindness.

J.O. Neill is a writer, creative producer and director, largely based in Bristol, UK. Born and raised till aged nine in Jamaica, her work is often concerned with themes of memory, history and belonging, strongly underpinned by a reverence for nature. She's written, produced and directed two independent, crowd-funded films, and is currently working on an essay collection, and an archive research project regarding an 18th century shipwreck. jessicaolivianeill.com; IG @jessolivianeill; Substack @jessolivianeill

Jana van Niekerk is a South African writer who lived away from her homeland until she was twelve years old. At seventeen she began publishing her experiences in short stories and poetry. In her matric exam she wrote a creative essay about having had a nomadic childhood, with all its ill and wondrous effects. Ironically it won the national Queen Victoria Memorial Prize.

Dike Nwosu is a poet, a screenwriter and university graduate born and raised in London, of Nigerian heritage. He writes provocative, thought-provoking poems with apocalyptic insights. A custodian of urban folklore, his writing explores the diaspora and the space where the street and Spirit interface. Very passionate about his poetry, he uses it as therapy and as a conduit to address profound questions and provide a communal space for people to delve deeper into the realms of knowledge and understanding of a fallen world.

Takunda G Nyika is a Zimbabwean writer, poet and playwright. His works have appeared in the Afterpast Review, Writers Space Africa and Inkundla Magazine. All poems to his name, including these herein and anywhere else are part of his yet to be published anthology *Fading Colours*. Takunda's works major on the political and socio-cultural imagination and experience of Africa and in particular Zimbabwe. Takunda says his works are a break from the writers of yore, African writers of the 20th century, whose work he identifies as radical and that he is ushering in a new era of moderatism in African literature. He is working with other like-minded youthful authors to create the Zimbabwe Youth Authors Federation (ZIYAF). Takunda is also a law student with a biased interest towards Business and Corporate Law, Economics and African jurisprudence in Constitutional Law.

Joseph C Ogbonna is a prolific poet from Nigeria. He has published very widely in magazines, anthologies, journals, and in online blogs. He was aired by the BBC Radio 3 for the bicentenary of the death of Napoleon Bonaparte on May the 5th, 2021. He lives in Enugu, Nigeria.

Educated at Ibadan and Syracuse Universities, **Tanure Ojaide** has published twenty-five collections of poetry, as well as four novels, five short story collections, three memoirs, and fourteen self-authored and co-authored scholarly books. He has won the Association of Nigerian Authors' Poetry Prize four times (1988, 1994, 2003, and 2011). His other awards include the Commonwealth Poetry Prize for the Africa Region (1988), the All-Africa Okigbo Prize for Poetry (1988), and the BBC Arts and Africa Poetry Award (1988). Ojaide is currently the Frank Porter Graham Distinguished Professor of Africana Studies at the University of North Carolina, Charlotte.

Dike Okoro was a finalist for Greece's Eyelands International Book Award. His poetry has been featured in *Witness Magazine*, *The Bellingham Review* (New Writing from Africa), *Obama Menthum: An Anthology of Transformational Poetry*, *Fingernails Across the Chalkboard: Poetry and Prose on HIV/AIDS from the Black Diaspora*, *Commutlit.com*, *Zocalo Poets*, and *Callaloo*. He is the author of the poetry collections *In the Company of the Muse*, *Homecoming: New and Selected Poems*, and *Dance of the Heart*.

Victor Ola-Matthew tells stories through multiple art forms. His work has appeared in the 2022 Afritondo anthology *Rain Dance*, and in BrittlePaper, and The Republic.

Omotayo Olaoye is a Chartered Accountant, African philosopher, author, poet, and songwriter. He is passionate about helping people develop the right attitude and deploy their potential and God-inspired ideas into profitable ventures. www.olaoyeonline.com.ng

Frank Olunga is a Kenyan poet born in 1999. He writes not only to inspire but see the world through poetic lenses. He is a teacher of English and literature and most of his works can be found in his blog masterworkpoetry.wordpress.com. As a poet he believes that poetry can change the world.

Alexander Opicho is a poet, essayist, short story writer, cultural critic and human rights crusader. He comes from Kenya.

Omobola Osamor's poetry examines the intersection of relationships—both human and institutional—and the emotions that arise from failures and successes. Her work, which includes poetry and fiction, has been featured in a range of publications, including Brittle Paper, African Writer, The Shallow Tales Review, and Flash Fiction Magazine. Born and raised in Lagos, Nigeria, she currently lives in Chicago.

Annette Pateman grew up in the UK, listening to African folklore told by her parents. Her poetry centres on Black identity, race and relationships. Annette is currently studying for an MA Creative Writing. She enjoys giving readings of her poetry, yoga, walking in nature, travelling and films.

Elly Ray is a poet from Hargeisa, Somalia. She has been writing as a hobby since childhood, she's a counselor, a word magician and a healer who took her journey healing and wishes to bring some healing upon the wounded among us.

Eric Rugara is a writer and editor. He is the author of two books *Broken Rhythm* and most recently *A Surreal Journey of Discovery*. His work has appeared in *Ibua Journal, Shallow Tales, The Elephant, Sisi Afrika* and *Qazini*. He has been published in a number of anthologies including *Flash Fiction International: Very Short Stories from Around the World*, and *In the Sands of Time* (Toyin Falola prize inaugural anthology), and in the 15th issue of *Flash* (University of Chester).

Mudadi Saidi is a World Summit Awards (WSA) Youth Ambassador, an independent researcher, and a passionate refugee advocate. He is also a Funding Futures contest laureate, and presented at Art for Peace in Washington D.C. in 2023. His writing has appeared in publications that include Catalyst Now. <https://www.linkedin.com/in/Mudadi-Saidi>

Deborah Saki is a Ghanaian writer and researcher whose work explores identity, displacement, memory, and power. She is a PhD candidate at Georgia State University, where she researches ethnic recognition and nation-building in post-conflict states. Her poetry and creative nonfiction have appeared or are forthcoming in *Brevity, IceFloe Press, Glassworks, The Kalahari Review*, and other journals. Her public writing has appeared in the *Times Higher Ed* and *Inside Higher Ed*. She lives between worlds—academic and artistic, research and reflection—and is committed to writing that bridges public and personal truths.

Inspired by his late elder brother Sankar Sarkar and his friends, especially Deb Kumar Khan, **Partha Sarkar**, a resident of Ichapur, a small town in the province of West Bengal in India and a graduate, writes poems to protest against social injustice and crimes against nature. His poems have been featured in different magazines both in Bangla and in English. Once, he believed in revolution but now he is confused because of human beings. Despite this, he keeps fire in the soul.

James Sentiba is an openly queer poet, writer, and blogger from Kampala, Uganda. His blog, senti-entertainment.com, is a personal entertainment blog dedicated to discussing representation in media and literature from an Afro-queer perspective. He is currently completing his bachelor's in film and media studies at Arizona State University.

Ndaba Sibanda is a Bulawayo-born poet, novelist and nonfiction writer who has authored thirty-four published books of various genres and persuasions and co-authored more than 100 published books.

Palmwine Sounds is a pseudonym of a Nigerian author of poetry and short stories that explore themes of love, loss, resilience, and spirituality. Their work is rooted in Nigeria but resonates globally. Palmwine Sounds poems tend to draw from the Rastafarian ideology.

Cindy Steward is an author and neuroscience graduate with Nigerian heritage. She has been writing stories and poetry since childhood. Her debut book, *Memoria of a Heart*, was published in 2020, and since then she has published in several anthologies, such as the *African Voices Anthology* and *Songs of Revolution* by Sunday Mornings at the River.

SuAndi is a writer, poet and arts practitioner born and raised in Manchester by a Liverpool Irish mother and a Nigerian Ijaw father. Her performances have taken her the length and breadth of the UK and out into Europe, North America, Brazil and into Africa. Her acclaimed one-woman show 'The Story of M' is now on the "A" Level curriculum. She has produced films on the Pan African 1945 congress, The Victorian Writer Ruskin and two historical accounts of African migrants to England from 1925 and Mothers of Mixed Race children. She is the recipient of an OBE, a Doctor of Arts from Manchester Metropolitan University and a Doctor of Letters degree from Lancaster University. Profiles of her life in the arts can be found on the Museum of Colour and Writer's Mosaic websites and the recently launched digital resource SussedBlackWoman. SuAndi received the Royal Society of Literature 2024 Benson Medal.

Sheila Thadani is a freelance writer and a poet. She has a Masters degree in Political Science and was a columnist for *Hi-Rise* magazine. Her articles have appeared in Substack. Her poetry has been published in *The Wave-Kelp Journal*, *Tiny Seed Journal*, Micromance, Poetryfest, DoubleSpeak, *A Song, Emerging Earth* (Studio Kroner and Just Earth Cincinnati, 2025) and Flicker Anthologies. Sheila has won prizes for her poems, "The Moral Abyss," "Quest for Peace," and "The Weeping Earth."

Patrick Kapuya Tshiuma is a software developer and father of 4 living and working in Israel with a refugee status obtained in 2004.

Philisiwe Twijnstra, a South African award-winning theatremaker, playwright, screenwriter, and fiction writer, recently emigrated to The Netherlands. She explores humanity's experiences, focusing on black narratives and inclusive representation, creating spaces for diverse voices, and capturing the richness of often marginalized human experiences through storytelling.

Ijeoma Victory Ejme is a Nigerian born writer, award winning poet, essayist and editor. Her works have appeared in the critique magazine, the Alias amongst others. She concerns herself with the issues of modern societies and a rapidly changing world.

Born and raised in Zimbabwe, **Faresi Yasini** lives in South Africa and is a Mechanical Technology teacher.

Gorrety Yogo is an early career researcher on Migration and Development. Gorrety enjoys writing, self-care and compassion during her personal time. She has self-published lots of note-books on self-care and one book on youth development on Amazon. Gorrety has been published by different projects on MIAG, Dynamig, IOM and the youth Cafe.

Furaha Youngblood was born in Shreveport, Louisiana and given the name Elizabeth Ann Youngblood. She grew up in Watts, a district of South Central Los Angeles and took the circuitous route in completing her education, eventually earning a Masters Degree in Broadcast Communications Art, and a Secondary Teaching credential. These were the tools she used to teach on the international education circuit – Tunisia, la Côte dÍvoire, Panama – from 1992 to 2008. The experiences she gained became the foundation for her evolution as a writer. As a broadcast journalist, from 1972 to 1979, her professional name was Furaha Hiyati ("Joy of my life").

Kathy Zwick taught history and social studies in several international schools. Sometimes she thinks she has learned more from her many international students than they ever learned from her.

ACKNOWLEDGEMENTS

Some of the poems in this anthology have been published previously as follows –

"Covered by Prayer" by Zan V. Johns, in *A Safe & Brave Space Anthology of Poetry and Art* (Garden of Neuro Publishing, 2021) and *After the Rainbow: Golden Poems* (Prolific Pulse Press LLC Publishing, 2022)

"you're always going" by Anton Krueger, in *New Contrast* in 2017 as part of a prose memoir essay titled "You're always going and coming…"

"Preparation for Lampedusa" by Octavia McBride-Ahebee, on *Octavia McBride-Ahebee: Eyes on the World; A Blog Ideas and the Arts*. Available at <https://omcbride-ahebee.blogspot.com/2014/08/preparations-for-voyage-to-lampedusa-by.html> [accessed: 1 February 2025], and in audio form on *Rattle Magazine*'s podcast: <https://m.facebook.com/RattlePoetry/videos/barbara-crooker-rattlecast-23-rebroadcast/476361029946109/> [accessed: 1 February 2025] (1 hr 1 min 20 secs in, to 1 hr 6 mins 30 secs)

"1822/2014" by Octavia McBride-Ahebee, in the online journal *Rigorous*, Issue 1 Volume 1. Available at: <https://www.rigorous-mag.com/v1i1/octavia-mcbride-ahebee.html> [accessed: 1 February 2025]

"The Isthmus That Splits Us" by Karuna Mistry, in Karuna Mistry's *You-me-verse-all Hueman* (Independently published, 2025)

"A Greater Loss" by Jenny Mitchell, a Trio International Competition prize winner, first published by *Culture Matters*

"Echoes of a Migrant's Ritual" by Fauziyatu 'Fauzi' Moro, was read at the Light Factory Publication's *Reading the Migration Library* public event in November 2021 under the title "Skin Map" and subsequently featured in the *Reading Diaspora/Reading Migration* interactive media project by students from Simon Fraser University in Canada.

"The B(lack)ody As a Map to Self" by Mariam Mohammed, in *Journal of African Youth Literature,* Issue 9. Available at <http://jaylit.com/issue-9/> [accessed: 10 September 2025]

"Where do I come?" by Mariam Mohammed, in *The Red Branch Review*, Issue 4 "st georges walks into a pub" by Ambrose Musiyiwa, in 21st Century Poetry, *Morning Star*, 17 September 2025. Available at: <https://morningstaronline.co.uk/article/st-georges-walks-pub> [accessed: 22 September 2025]

"A New City" by Deborah Saki, in *On-the-High Literary Journal*

'III', in "Blood and Sugar of Home" by Deborah Saki, as "Intentions", in *Tampered Press*

"Intergenerational Trauma" by SuAndi, in SuAndi's *Leaning Against Time* (Carcanet Press, 2025)

"Fountain of Furry" by Zainab M. Hassan, initially part of a very long poem titled "The Ruin," originally published in *Horn of Africa Journal: An Independent Journal* (2011), Volume XXX, pages 116-125, Rutgers University, Newark, NJ. A revised version later appeared in *Bildhaan: An International Journal of Somali Studies*, (2020), Vol. 20, Article 10, pages 84-97, Macalester College, St. Paul, Minnesota, available online at <https://digitalcommons.macalester.edu/cgi/viewcontent.cgi?article=1228&context=bildhaan> [accessed: 14 November 2025]

"Another Man's Land", by Victor Ola-Matthew, in *Brittle Paper* in 2022.

"Ours Is An Unbreakable Love" by Ndaba Sibanda, as part of "3 Poems by Ndaba Sibanda" in *The Fictional Café*, 3 June 2024. Available at <https://fictionalcafe.com/3-poems-by-ndaba-sibanda/> [accessed: 19 April 2025]

"As Long As" by Ndaba Sibanda, in the *Calla Press Literary Journal*. Available at <https://www.callapresspublishing.com/literaryjournal/as-long-as-by-ndaba-sibanda> [accessed: 19 April 2025]

"Screams and Streams of Splendor" by Ndaba Sibanda, in *Written Tales Magazine*, 3 May 2022. Available at <https://writtentales.substack.com/p/screams-and-streams-of-splendor> [accessed: 19 April 2025]

"Kunta Kinte" by Palmwine Sounds, in Palmwine Sounds' *Life and Death: Part 2* (Palmwine Publishing, 2025)

"The Green, Red, Black and Gold" by Palmwine Sounds, in Palmwine Sounds' *Music and Life: Rasta Vibrations* (Palmwine Publishing, 2025)

ABOUT THE POETRY ANTHOLOGY SERIES

Organised by Forced Migration and The Arts in collaboration with CivicLeicester and Regularise, the Africa Migration Report Poetry Anthology Series draws inspiration from the 2nd Edition of the *Africa Migration Report*[1], jointly published by the African Union Commission (AUC) and the International Organization for Migration (IOM) in March 2024.

The poetry anthology series differs from the report in that, through poetry, the anthology series explores multifaceted narratives, capturing personal, familial, community, national and international histories, experiences, hopes, dreams and aspirations around African and African diasporic migration.

We take the African diaspora to include all people of African descent in all the ways they define themselves, e.g. African, African-Caribbean, African American, Afro Asian, Afro Brazilian, Afro Latino, Afropean, Black British, Black, etc.

Because every day is Africa Day, our call for submissions[2] is open 365 days a year.

About The Organisers

Forced Migration and The Arts is an international network that brings together people with lived experience of forced migration, refugee and non-refugee artists, academics and art spaces for conversation looking at work taking place at the intersection where forced migration and the arts meet. The network, initial stages of which were developed with support from the University of Manchester's Humanities Global Scholars Fund, hosts monthly indabas[3] or conversations, usually on the last Thursday of each month, and encourages mutual support and collaboration.

---

[1] African Union (2024). Press Release. Africa Migration Report: Linking policy, practice and the welfare of the African migrant Internal: Africa Migration Report. African Union, 26 March. Available at: <https://au.int/en/pressreleases/20240326/africa-migration-report-linking-policy-practice-and-welfare-african-migrant> [Accessed: 5 November 2025]
[2] Forced Migration and The Arts. (2025). Open Call for Submissions - The Africa Migration Report: An Anthology of Poems. Forced Migration and The Arts blog, 25 January. Available at: <https://forcedmigrationandthearts.blogspot.com/2025/01/open-call-for-submissions-africa.html> [Accessed: 11 November 2025]
[3] A playlist of videos from some of the conversations held as part of Forced Migration and The Arts is available here: <https://www.youtube.com/watch?v=6o_QRTW55r0&list=PL-kiEIc_8yhRIA2UBrwB8wgSTcJZ5Q0Da&index=2> [Accessed: 19 October 2024]

Regularise[4] is a migrant-led collective founded in late 2019, prior to the COVID-19 pandemic. The collective aims to address the years of sustained hardship that undocumented migrants experience in the UK and continues to organise and campaign for justice and for the rights of undocumented migrants.

CivicLeicester[5] is a community publisher that uses print and digital technologies, social media platforms, the arts, and online and in-person events to highlight conversations of transnational interest and significance. Books CivicLeicester has published include *Black Lives Matter: Poems for a New World* (2023), *Welcome to Britain: An[other] Anthology of Poems and Short Fiction* (2022), and *Bollocks to Brexit: An Anthology of Poems and Short Fiction* (2019).

Approach

We would like to publish the poems in the Africa Migration Report Poetry Anthology Series in ways that are slightly different from how poetry anthologies tend to be published and are very much looking forward to working with you as part of the process. The ideas we are working with are (and we look forward to your thoughts on these):

Starting in October 2024, we will be hosting a rolling series of online and in-person poetry events at which poets who have submitted material for possible inclusion in the anthology series will meet to read and talk about their work and share thoughts, experiences, reflections and hopes, dreams and aspirations around African and African diasporic migration.

Each session will be between an hour to two hours long, and will be free and open to all. Each session will be recorded and posted on the website we are building around the initiative.

Each recording will then be broken down, so that we post each poet reading and contextualising their poems as a block (e.g. if a poet talks about and reads three poems, this will be posted as a standalone segment). Where a poet has read more than one poem, each poem will also be presented as a standalone poem, maybe with a contextualisation, maybe without.

To each of the poems, we would also like to add audio-visual representations inspired by the poem. Examples of these include photographs, paintings, or multimedia installations, music or soundscapes inspired by the poems, and geospatial mapping where we would use Geographic Information Systems (GIS) to map routes or places mentioned in the poems. We would also like to overlay these routes or places with historical data, population density, cultural landmarks and other details.

---

[4] https://regularise.org/
[5] https://www.facebook.com/CivicLeicester/

And where the poem mentions historical figures, we would like to add photos, biographical details and other audio-visual representations. After a sufficient number of poets have read and discussed their poems, and before or after they have been published on the website, we would then like to publish the paperback editions.

The Paperback Editions

Each paperback issue or edition in the poetry anthology series will feature 63 poets. Each poet will be encouraged to contribute three poems or more. Each poet will also be encouraged to contribute to three collaborative poems on the following themes: "Africa 2063", "The Africa We Want" and "Africa 2100".

In this, we are riffing off the African Union's *Agenda 2063: The Africa We Want*[6], so that, in this way, we draw attention to The Agenda. In this way, we also tie the experiences, concerns, expectations, hopes, dreams and aspirations that the poets and artists are sharing around African migration to that agenda as well.

In addition, with the collaborative poems, we invite poets and artists to be unfettered in imagining, envisaging and expressing possible and better futures for Africans on the continent, in the diaspora and on the move.

With each issue or edition, we would also like to ensure that the cover, like the anthologies themselves, features artwork from Africans on the continent, in the diaspora and on the move.

We are also aiming to include those living in formal and informal refugee camps and settlements, in ghettos and in slums, on-grid and off-grid, on the streets, in prisons and detention centres, and in cities, towns and villages on the continent and around the world.

Aim and Purpose

With each print edition, we would like to call for a world in which, contrary to what is happening at present, the rights of African migrants are respected and protected, and in which freedom of movement extends to and includes Africans on the continent, in the diaspora and on the move.

---

[6] https://au.int/en/agenda2063/overview

We are also hoping that each edition will include an introduction by a different, contemporary pan-African thinker. Examples we can think of include the former AU ambassador to the UN, Dr. Arikana Chihombori-Quoa, and people like PLO Lumumba, Joshua Maponga, Brian Kagoro, Julius Malema, and David Oliver Yambio. If you know of other contemporary pan-African thinkers we should be paying attention to and invite to introduce the poetry, please let us know and we will look them up and see if we can work with them and them with us.

The hope is that, this way, we keep the poetry, the conversations, the music, the art and the demands going for as long as it takes for change to happen. The hope is also that, in this way, we encourage more artists, on the continent, in the diaspora and on the move to engage with the theme and the issues, so that we get to hear their perspectives and views on the matter, both through the art they are making and through the poetry and the conversations.

In doing this, we would also like to centre the orality that marks poetry as it has been practised on the continent and in the African diaspora for centuries and millennia. We would also like to centre and work with the potential and capacity that poetry and the arts have to keep memory and knowledge alive as well as their capacity to bring people together and how this coming together can lead to action and necessary change.

We would like to encourage Africans on the continent, in the diaspora and on the move to meet more and connect with each other more, and talk to each other more about issues that affect us, starting with questions around the regime that governs African migration and mobility.

As referenced in the AU/IOM's *Africa Migration Report: 2nd Edition*, the continent is currently working towards setting up a free movement infrastructure similar to or better than that which is in place in the European Union. Related to this, we hope that the poetry anthology series, in all the forms that it will take, will encourage Africans on the continent, in the diaspora and on the move to take part in the conversation that is taking place on the continent and in the diaspora on the matter.

We also hope that the anthology series will encourage the African Union and countries on the continent to pick up the pace on the plans, and ensure that freedom of movement is a right that Africans on the continent, in the diaspora and on the move can enjoy alongside all the rights identified in the African Charter on Human and People's Rights, including the right to freedom from discrimination (Articles 2 and 18(3)), freedom from cruel, inhuman and degrading treatment and punishment (Article 5), the right to life and personal integrity (Article 4), and the right to dignity (Article 5).

Funding

Currently, the Africa Migration Report Poetry Anthology Series is unfunded and is being fuelled by volunteer energy and individual and collective resources at our disposal. We have set up a crowdfunding appeal[7] and welcome and are open to suggestions on how we can fund the initiative.

Editorial Board

Advisory Board

Contact Person

aj maruva
Editorial Assistant, Africa Migration Report Poetry Anthology Series
E: forcedmigrationandthearts@gmail.com

---

[7] https://gofund.me/294ad2b

Japa Fire: An Anthology of Poems on African and African Diasporic Migration
Eds. Ambrose Musiyiwa and Munya R

'All told, this anthology is a great introduction to a range of political African voices you won't come across in many other places.' – Ruth Aylett, in *The Morning Star*

Black Lives Matter: Poems for a New World
Ed. Ambrose Musiyiwa

'With over 100 contributions from writers of diverse ages and backgrounds, the collection is a poignant exploration of an era of renewed protest and newfound solidarities, against the backdrop of the coronavirus pandemic. [...] The revolutionary task of overturning imperialism cannot be achieved, the collection suggests, by appealing to those with power. Black Lives Matter: Poems for a New World *urges its readers to take matters into our own hands if we truly want to build this new world.'* – Ananya Wilson-Bhattacharya, in *The Norwich Radical*

Bollocks to Brexit: An Anthology of Poems and Short Fiction
Ed. Ambrose Musiyiwa

'This is an anthology that wears its heart on its sleeve. Clad (perhaps not uncoincidentally) in Liberal Democrat yellow, it brings together an eclectic range of voices against Brexit, from established poets and spoken word performers to flash fiction writers and lyricists. [...] The contributors are motivated by feelings of sorrow, anger, frustration and alienation, and the anthology itself seems intended to offer a kind of therapy both to the authors and the presumed audience.' – David Clarke, in *Sabotage Reviews*